# Can Communicate Christ

*Charlotte Ostermann*

*Catholics Communicate Christ*

Copyright 2023 © Charlotte Ostermann

All rights reserved. No part of this book may be reproduced or transmitted in any form or by any means, electronic or mechanical, including photocopying, recording, or by any information storage and retrieval system, without the written permission from the author, except for the inclusion of brief quotations in a review.

MotherheartPress.com

Cover design, book formatting by Gina Laiso, Integrita Productions

ISBN-13: 978-1-7321037-4-0

Printed in the United States

# Table of Contents

Introduction ....................................................................... 5

## Section I – Communication Flourishes in Community

Chapter 1 – The Church is the Context of Christ ........... 13

Chapter 2 – Persons are Form, Rising ............................ 39

Chapter 3 – Conversation: Context for Truth ................ 59

Chapter 4 – Communication Science in Light of Christ .. 81

## Section II – Communication is a Collaboration

Chapter 5 – We-They: Love is the Context ................. 105

Chapter 6 – Rhetoric for the New Evangelization ........ 131

Chapter 7 – Evangelization as Argument .................... 145

Chapter 8 – The Arts of Communication .................... 161

## Section III – Newness is the Glory of God, Form is the Filament

Chapter 9 – Renewing the Culture .............................. 179

Chapter 10 – In Conversation with Culture ................. 199

Chapter 11 – The Possibilities of Form ....................... 229

Chapter 12 – Recapitulation of the Human Person ...... 251

Thank you to the friends and family members who have spent real time with me, shared your lives with me, borne me up in prayer, and entrusted me with your deepest concerns. This book has been written in the midst of us – in hundreds of hours of conversation among the two-or-more who become a vessel for Christ's Presence. Thus is the Presence made ever-new in us, and thus is Christ communicated into the world. I hope you will hear echoes of all our conversations within these pages.
May the Word dwell in you richly!

Love, Charlotte

# Introduction

This book is a call to Catholics to be more fully realized as communicators of Christ, after the pattern of Christ.

Christ communicates Himself 'down' into the Church, the context that nurtures Christ-life. Thus, He is incorporated into a people, who become, individually, instances of Christ, or seed: the content that re-presents Him. As she grows up, the Church-receptive becomes the Church-expressive – form that, by standing for Christ stands against anything anti-Christ. As Church infills with form – with people, encyclicals, traditions, etc… – she becomes a richer and richer context-within-which persons are nurtured and formed to communicate Christ. Persons, within her, grow up to form new contexts-of-being and, together, become knitted together as a Body – an interior life of community, belonging, we-ness, and with-ness. This rich interiority invites all who are not yet with-Christ into companionship with Him.

The Church-as-form-and-life (content-and-context, sacrament-and-substance, organization-and-organism) becomes a more and more fully developed interface (a 'both-and,' or 'two-way' form) by means of which Christ communicates Himself out, 'horizontally,' or 'universally' in space-time so as to be communicated and realized in all people, times, and places. The continuous 'vertical' and 'horizontal' communication of Christ to the world is powered by Love, and occurs in the context of Love – the interior life of the Trinity, which is mirrored in our community life. The imperfect forms generated by the interaction between His perfection and the flaws in His 'materials' serve, imperfectly, to communicate Him and, in that work – in that movement or process – are shaken, flooded, found wanting, and are continuously renewed and remade to stand, fitter and firmer *as* forms against the pull of chaos and disorder around them.

The work of the Word is both transitive – moving outward from Christ through form – and intransitive – accomplishing growth and change within the vessels which carry it. The action of the Word – the communication of Christ – is the realization of Christ in, to an ever-expanding degree, the world of form. By means of Christ-realized-in-form, all created form is meant to be returned to God, fulfilled. By a simple pattern of *exitus-reditus* (Word, going out and returning), the unimaginable complexity of a universe fulfilled in *every* particular is to occur, is occurring, and will (at time's end) have perfectly and wholly occurred. It is 'unimaginable' because only the mind of God could remotely comprehend it. Yet it is given to the mind of man to approach it analogically and even to participate in it directly at the scale of 'personhood'.

The ever-expanding degree to which Christ is realized depends at once upon the two directions of communication: a) The degree to which the form, vessel, or material is receptive to, or able to receive and appropriate Christ, and b) The degree to which the form, vessel, or material is able truthfully, fully, effectively to express, or disseminate Christ. A both-and, two-way, vertical-and-horizontal interfacial form must develop through some both-and, two-way, vertical-and-horizontal movement. Communication of Christ is such a movement for the continuous growth of the Church, of the person, and of any further forms we make. Communication thus understood is a way of working creatively to resolve tensions, of fighting against the pull of extremes into chaos or complacency, of struggling to work out our salvation, of growing up spirally in a movement that often feels distressingly circular, and of finding power in smallness and greatness in powerlessness.

Failure in capacity (to be/to generate adequate context), or in ability (to be/to generate adequate content) is not a stopping place, or barrier to the communication of Christ, but is information provided and usable for the growth-in-integrity, edification, or strengthening of His people – the forms within and by means of which Christ is communicated. Failure is inevitable, but as feedback that continuously improves the system of communication, is invaluable.

The task is three-fold: understanding the mission, practicing the skills, and recovering capacity for Christ. The results should also be three-fold: a human person strengthened by freedom to bear the weight of glory; a Church healed by unity to become a context for encounter with Christ; a Kingdom emerging through conversation to voice Christ's response to the realities met through His people. Communicating Christ is not an exclusively sacramental exchange, though this is the highest form it may take, in time. Christ is communicated through the existence of every created being; through bearers of His presence, small and large, scarred and beautiful; through His Body the Church, in her rituals, liturgy and literature, community and conversation, symbols and substances;

through both manifold context and structured emptiness which give rise to the rich indwelling of the Word; through the silent radiance of beauty, the carefully crafted utterance of art, and the proclamation of the Church. Christ is communicated through form: the human person and his words, gestures, acts and works. Christ is communicated through relationship – the practice of the presence of persons: in the community of families and friends, Church and civil society.

Communication is a movement from God, toward God, that occurs through the Church by God's design. Communication, at its best, possesses and radiates the primary quality of Love, which drapes the Mystery in perceptibility so that we may sense its action. Love is the first Reality that touches and awakens the "I" of the human person, and the sound or glimpse of glory that continues to call him through every created reality toward his destiny. In the movement that is 'communication,' a person, a people, a Church, a Kingdom interface emerges, rises, becomes realized, is formed. The intransitive work of 'communication' accomplishes the realization of Christ into the world not as a 'message,' or an 'ethos,' but as a person, as a Presence within a people. We communicate Christ by *being* full of Him, *becoming* like Him, voicing His response to the realities we encounter and resounding the Word at our origin, which is joyful praise to God for *being*, itself. Communication, then, is a complex, multi-faceted, polyvalent symphony of resounding Christ universally until we are forms-fully-realized and returned to eternal intimacy with one another and with our Creator. It is also a simple, elegant pattern of *exitus-reditus*, or call-and-response – the lemniscate motion of the Holy Spirit who is Love – by which, and within which all created being participates in a movement of following and finding fulfillment in Christ.

*Catholics Communicate Christ* is the beginning of a conversation about a fully Catholic theory of communication. Such a theory cannot be abstract, merely conceptual, or academic, but must be a 'living lens' through which to focus on and through and toward the human person, who is the image of God. Seeing him, we see how Christ, communicated, is Christ realized more and more fully in reality, in time and space, in actuality. Seeing him, we see what it means to rescue and restore human persons by the light of Christ, communicated. Seeing him, we get a glimpse of the glory God veils in form.

"Communicating Christ" suggests at once the least-possible-form to convey the greatest-possible meaning, and the richest-possible context for the simplest-possible message. The free human person is such a form, as is the Church which Christ is creating with our co-operation. Ultimately, we will see, I think, that the Kingdom of God is such a form, as well. 'Person' is, becomes, and will ultimately be perfected, and given place in the Divine Communion of Persons, in the movement between being and becoming *imago Dei*. The Church was born, is growing up, and will ultimately have perfectly matured in the movement between being and becoming Bride – both womb of the emerging Christ and structure resounding the Word within her. The Kingdom has come, is emerging, and will ultimately prevail over all anti-person, anti-*logos*, anti-God structures as Christ is fully realized to consummate perfect union with perfect vessel in the accomplishment of infinite, eternal fulfillment-in-form of all that is "I AM." Amen!

A Catholic theory of communication is an impossibility, in a way, as it seeks to provide an overarching-and-underpinning context for situating ourselves in the vast story of God's own communication of Himself. At the same time, it aspires to provide an infrastructural support for participation in the action of that self-communication of God. Yet, because through small and foolish things God gives access to Himself, such a theory may be sketched upon the matrix of Holy Wisdom which is, in fact, that context and that structure. A fully 'grown up' theory would have to touch upon theology far beyond this book's scope, and to wrestle with the human 'science of communication' in detail far beyond this book's scope. So, please, accept this conversation, this small sketch, as the little 'lens' it hopes to be. Perhaps you will be called upon to develop it more fully.

Communication science has developed from a simplistic understanding of communication as 'successfully transferring a message from one person to another,' to a more nuanced and complex understanding of communication as 'effectively transmitting meaning through means that, themselves, may both distort and amplify that meaning.' The 'problem' has become not just adequately encoding then decoding a message, but also considering the contexts of personal experience, literary allusion, various interpretations of symbol systems, and many other contextual factors that affect transmission of the message itself. A Catholic communication theory leaves behind the rather two-dimensional plane of the problem of getting a message across, in favor of a more three-dimensional model in which the means themselves (the messengers, vessels, symbols, or forms by means of which meaning is conveyed) are affected by the Message communicating Himself through them.

The transformation of form from empty to full, from dead to alive, from false to true, from opaque-and-obscuring-truth to translucent-and-radiating-the-beauty-of-truth is the newness made possible by the indwelling Person of Christ. We believers co-operate in the reception and expression of Christ, and are improved as means for communicating Him in the process. As the perfect Artist, perfecting materials into form that accords with both their own nature and with His Idea, Christ is bringing about the fulfillment of each instrument, so that we each are promised our own particular realization, fulfillment, and destiny.

A simple statement of a Catholic theory of communication is "Catholics communicate Christ." From here, we can put out into the deep to consider the context, the content, the science and skills, and the art of communicating Christ.

Chapter 1

# The Church is the Context of Christ

The Word became flesh and generated a Body, a people, a Church by means of which to give himself to the world. His coming was, itself, a response to the reality of the being of God; a first and final form in which the I Am expressed himself as the utterance of all form, all being, returned as the perfect fulfillment of all that is. The work of the Church occurs within this overarching self-communication of God and in light of His own perfect fulfillment of Himself. No Church, no work, is needed to complete Him, to finish His work, or to give meaning to the forms He created. Yet the Church is invited – mankind is invited – onto the stage, or the playground, where the Spirit moves in unceasing delight through the arc of *exitus-reditus*: going out and coming in to express and trace and resound the Word God has uttered; echoing and filling with ultimate significance the Word at the origin of all being; calling constantly for our participation in the love of the Trinity, and leading us toward the Word who is our destiny.

I cannot understand my role in the communication of Christ without perceiving it within the context of the role of the Church. We tend to think of the Church as 'built up of persons,' but it is first the 'context in which free personhood is made possible' by the communication of Christ. The Church is the context of the possibility of persons.

**Middlework is the Mission of the Faithful**

We live in the 'between' of space-time, weaving the world together in the context of history, of man's becoming, of Christ's movement to fill every sign with meaning, and of the emergence of the Kingdom of God. Our task – to communicate Christ – could be called 'middlework': participation in the pattern of realizing Christ by moving deeper into communion with Him, which is also communion with His Body, the Church. His life takes shape as the gift of faith descends to fill the space of longing in an individual, generating Christ-life in each believer. As He grows, His people are woven into a membership that provides hopeful context for the continuous sharing of gifts – in liturgy and in lived community life. We become, together, a 'we': a people led by Christ to voice His love, His good news, His calling to freedom. Our faith blooms into an atmosphere of hope as we speak of Him – as Christ-in-His-Church – with one voice, truthfully and in love.

Absent this 'we,' each of us speaks alone and ineffectually. As a Body, we become an edifice, a vessel, a place, a form within which Christ-life is nurtured and grows up to engage with the wider world. The first form, or sign, to be restored to its meaning-fullness by Christ was human community, family, or belonging – all embodied in the Church. From its beginning, His Church was a true Sign of contradiction, of truth, of sacrifice. The earliest Church knew itself to be both human and divine, transmitting by supernatural power through natural beings the very Body, Blood, Soul and Divinity of the Word made flesh, made bread, made form. To some degree, the success of the mission – to communicate Christ – depends upon the unity of His members, the integrity of His Body, and the richness of communication within the Church – all of which contribute to the overflow, or resounding of Christ to the world around us.

To be 'within the Church' is to be couched in layers and layers of form that strengthen the individual structure to stand, and to become fully realized. The Sacraments, doctrine, organizational structure, history, creeds, rites and rituals, and people (dead and alive) that surround a Catholic person act as mediating structures to him for grace, truth, and the person of Christ. They hold him in being as he grows, and align him with the Holy Wisdom he is to embrace and share. He ingests the surrounding context, which becomes infrastructure within him that corresponds to the realities he encounters in the world. Rich context and strong verbal structure leads to act and thus to freedom, much as muscle action pulls the skeletal system into being to support physical freedom. Act becomes form as each believer generates his own gestures, verbal structures, and works of art. Form becomes new contexts as believers become friends, families, communities, institutions, welcoming events, and new instances of Church. Ideally, each new context will be resonant with the Truth that generated the Church, radiant with the Love that sustains her, and rich with forms that dispose people to receive grace.

The Church has 'good bones,' as we might say of an old, sound house that has the potential to be beautifully renovated. Those bones, hard and inert as they may seem, are active, living factories for the production of healing and cleansing blood. The life of the Body is in the Blood that flows through the structures of the Church. The structure of bones gives us a clue about the combination of substance and space within the Church. A skeleton of solid bone would be too heavy to provide freedom for the body it supports.

Real bone is a dense structure permeated by space, or space held open by sufficient structure. It is a kind of 'foam,' generated as substance is infused with an invisible something-else of another order. As gluten strands in flour are opened by incorporated gas from the growth of yeast, then cooked to become a solid 'foam' of delectable bread, so the Sabbath space of encounter with Christ is held in being by the substances and structure of the Church. That space, in each individual, might be called his spaciousness, or his interior freedom. Each person growing up in all things unto Christ follows the pattern of incorporating and then expressing the contexts that surround him. The community life of the Church might be thought of as the musculature of action and expression that develops so many different forms upon the deep, internal skeletal structure that supports freedom of movement and response.

The love that is meant to flow out to the world is meant, first, to circulate within the Body. Then, together, we – as Christ-in-His-Church – build and become a mediating structure through which – by means of which – He is communicated to others. As a people, a 'we', the Body shows the world our love for one another. To be 'within the Church' is also to be party to failures, or imperfections of that form. We clearly fail at living as a 'community of love, growing in Christ-likeness' (to quote St. Pope John Paul II's jubilee prayer for the Church). Why not look at and learn from that failure?

**Building Community**

It seems obvious that we Catholics should 'build community.' We know community is good, like we know 'art is good' – even without being completely clear what we mean by it, or what is good about it. It's really the idea of 'building' it, whatever it is, that feels hard and less positive. Understanding why it is important – to the Church and to the world – for us not only to theorize about, but also to practice community, should help motivate you past that resistance.

In my homeschooling years, I made a point of connecting with fellow parent-educators. One acquaintance, who avoided group events, once asked why I kept inviting her. "To help us build community," I replied. "Community? We don't need that. We're Catholic, and that makes us all one big community. That's enough for me." Her comments awakened me to a new reality. Not everyone longs for community as much as I do, or at least doesn't define it the same way! I felt embarrassed – briefly – to have brought Catholicity into question somehow. As a recent convert, I wondered if 'community' was a vaguely Protestant notion I should have left behind. Then I read Robert Putnam's *Bowling Alone*.[1]

Putnam researched dozens of seemingly unrelated measurements to find clues to a bigger picture of societal disintegration. From 'how many clubs are you in,' to 'how many kids on the block can you name,' to 'how many times per week does your family eat dinner together,' Putnam looked for measures of the civic engagement that produce a wealth he called 'social capital'. He found a clear pattern of decline over the 1900's in all things human and communital. That decline in the everyday, mundane, seemingly insignificant activities that weave together the fabric of life correlated with the obvious markers indicating the unraveling of that fabric – divorce rates, suicide rates, drop-out rates, etc... Left unsaid was the

---
[1] Robert Putnam, *Bowling Alone*.

equally obvious correlation of social decline with increase in the use of birth control.

"This book should be read by Catholics," I thought. "The Church could do so much, so simply, to help knit the world back together." And, yes, the Church could, but seems unequal to the task of rescuing those perishing on all sides – perhaps due to internal disintegration. On the one hand, there are Catholics with a desire to put faith into practice as good works – sometimes willing to leave the Church itself behind in the wake of zealous practical activity – and on the other hand are Catholics keeping orthodox doctrine and beautiful liturgy from violation, who sometimes forget the flood of need outside the Ark.

What's missing is a robust and resilient structure made of people – us – which allows for excellent communication between these poles in tension. Community is the mediating structure, the Body, through which Christ is placed into interaction with the world. If only our 'heads' interact with the world, the relationship becomes political. If only our 'hands' interact with the world, those we serve will not see the face of Christ. If the Church is to offer a 'full-bodied' response to the realities we encounter, she will need a well-knit body, blood, soul, and humanity.

This is the promise of "community," whatever form it takes. As we share Christ in our midst, He is amplified, in a sense, like a sound, like a word, and resounds more and more fully into the world. As we become His communicating interface with the world, we return that world to Him for blessing, for restoration and healing, for fulfillment. Back and forth the Spirit can move, unless we are each separate, isolated, disconnected entities – body parts unreconciled and thus unable to operate in harmony with the whole Body for the sake of the rest of humanity. Through Christ-in-His-Church, the isolation, despair, and loneliness that is arguably the number one threat to human life, can be overcome. None of us can address it alone, but together we become the living structure to whom all men are drawn by the light of Christ, dwelling within.

Who wouldn't want to become a part of a richly structured and supplied conduit for light and life to a hurting world? So, why don't we? Let's turn to the reasons we don't build community. There are as many, at least, as there are members of the Body, but I'll give you ten:

**Why We Don't**

*1. We Don't Want to be Affected*

We don't build community because we have become so flattened, so satisfied with virtual 'others,' and so accustomed to abstractions of reality that we've lost capacity for the intrusive, messy, unpredictable reality of other persons. Theory shines brightly, but practice threatens you with wounds, discomfort, and exposure of your weaknesses. I'm reminded of a small community building experiment I was involved with. After a year of planning, a few families created a homeschool cooperative.

So much common faith, so much like-mindedness, and so much good will went into this that I was baffled by the first unraveling thread. On day one it was discovered by one parent that another family allowed their children to bring Lunchables ™ to school. It wasn't enough to say that this was a matter of individual choice, whatever you thought about the nutritional value or environmental impact of Lunchables ™. It seemed unbearable that their children be in a situation that might so negatively affect their opinions about this lunch option – that their kids might now want such a thing, and that they would be put into a position of having to say no. The whole community was expected to bow to the expectation of lunch homogeneity. It never had occurred to me to prepare for a contingency this petty. I now realize how much personal formation, verbal preparation and smaller-scale practice would be needed before such an ambitious undertaking as a shared, family-style education community.

## 2. *We are Reduced by Reductionist Culture*

We don't build community because we are used to buying things ready-made and prefer to pay for rather than make them by planning and participation. We know how to come to programs someone makes for us to enjoy, but not how to build living structures as we inhabit them. But only a living structure is adequate for human becoming. Building community is the making of us as persons. Without this supportive structure, we lose scope for being fully realized as individuals.

## 3. *We Suffer from Survivor Guilt*

We don't build community because we feel 'survivor guilt'. Seeing all the riches and advantages we possess against the backdrop of poverty around us, we hesitate to generate even more wealth for ourselves – social capital, relationships, concerts, education – by building community. As an example, I heard a woman voice the opinion that she shouldn't read to her kids at home since so many schoolmates didn't have that advantage.

But, the rich get richer in wealth like this *for the sake of* those God asks them to serve. The overflow from their tables is meant to be channeled to those in need, to the glory of God. From those who "have not," everything will be taken – not because they aren't worthy of Gift, but because they gradually lose capacity to receive and hold onto it. To build community is to strengthen the capacity to hold on to and thus to transmit the goods we are given. Structure holds open space, conserves value, enables flow and distribution. The richest interfacial structure I can think of is the placenta, which mediates between mother and child, in both directions, proportioning Gift to be given and need to be communicated. The riches are given for the sake of re-gifting them, so we should cultivate more, not make do with less!

*4. We Lack Maturity*

We don't build community because we are waiting for leadership, experts trained in Community Building, people with credentials in pastoral ministry or parish administration – waiting for them to give permission, to lead, to create new programs and resources, to put the word out, to decide when and where, to send us a save-the-date, and to ask for our help as needed. But, thankful as we are for great leaders and church secretaries, the Church also must cultivate people who lead themselves – free men and women who act on their own initiative and in concert with the Church's teachings. If my grown children never got together except when I held a family reunion, it would show a lack of full growth into adulthood. We are children of the Church – docile and humble – and we are the world's adults – free and generative. Building community helps us to integrate those poles of our personal reality. Community is a matrix of support for growing up – offered to us, and as we grow up, offered to new Christians and persons at various removes from our own beliefs.

*5. We've Forgotten Holy Leisure*

We don't build community because we have *acedia* – a spiritual lassitude expressed both as laziness and as distracted busy-ness. We have difficulty just being – being at leisure with God, with self, and with others. We either focus on end results – on *doing* together – and downgrade the value of *being* together, or we expect common time to be pure fun, chill, relaxing: to make no demands. The cure for *acedia* is holy leisure – Sabbath-keeping that corresponds to human freedom, response-ability, and generativity.[2]

*6. We Have a Limited Understanding of Church*

We don't build community because we misunderstand 'Church' as a venue for recitals and potlucks, the priest as a Sacrament vending machine, spiritual communities as things only made by consecrated religious, and the worshippers around us as supporting cast members in a drama that ends with the curtain call, "Thanks be to God." But, as you know, the drama we're in doesn't end, the priest reifies Christ in our midst, the Church is the antechamber of Heaven, 'community' does not have to involve lifetime vows, and we actually *need* those other people to realize the Body of Christ fully.

*7. We're Frightened by Scary Images of Community*

We don't build community because it takes time and trust, desire and courage, strong faith and personal freedom to

---

[2] Charlotte Ostermann, *Souls at Rest – An Exploration of the Eucharistic Sabbath* and Charlotte Ostermann, *Sabbath Simplified*

do so, and we don't have enough. We wrongly assume that to build Catholic community requires spending our scant free time with people we fear, distrust, don't like, or have to help. We wrongly assume that we would have to say 'yes' to anything a community member asks of us. We wrongly imagine that a commitment to any form of community means a loss of personal freedom. While we are imagining community instead of building it, these images of what it would be like if we ever got involved with others cause an understandable aversion. But if we follow the Scripture's admonition to "cast down vain imaginings," and just respond in freedom to the person and realities we actually face in the moment, we'll find building community much less onerous than we wrongly imagined. We don't have the 'enough' of anything to build community – that's why it becomes practice for trusting in God's provision.

## 8. We are Polarized by Mistrust

We don't build community because we mis-trust anything 'grassroots,' 'horizontal,' or 'subjective/experiential/organic' as being from the pit of commie, progressive, new age, hippie hell. Or, we mis-trust anything 'hierarchical,' 'vertical,' 'superior,' or 'objective/theological/organized' as being from the pit of medieval, regressive, authoritarian, aristocrat hell. We divide ourselves by political affiliation, school of choice, theological camp, mask preference, vaccine status, modesty level, pious practice scores – anything will keep us conveniently at arm's length from the possibility of being uncomfortably affected by another person. We suspect that any movement toward another's position is a relativist compromise. We are looking for what C.S. Lewis called an "inner ring" – an exclusive – and so, safe – place of special belonging.[3] But such rings,

---

[3] C.S. Lewis, *The Inner Ring*

by nature, get smaller and smaller as they reduce us in scope and power. They get dangerous as they turn in upon themselves.

## 9. We've Developed Flattened Notions of Economy

We don't build community because we are immersed in an economy of exchange, of cost-benefit analysis, and of obligations that may be discharged by the abstraction we call 'money'. We have not practiced participating in the Economy of Gift, which is a much better pre-text for the Economy of Grace. Gift generates a unique tension: the obligation to be grateful. It also generates a unique opportunity: the chance to reciprocate, which multiplies the Gift. Both this in-tension and this ex-tension can only be resolved in freedom, by a free human person (who may need to ask for a reasonable fee). Thus the Economy of Gift invites us to exercise and expand our freedom. In community, we have small-scale practice of resolving these tensions, and examples from real life of the different ways others resolve them. Community is a micro-economic preview of the great macro-economics of grace. We dare not reduce it to a comfortable system of arm's length transaction, or equal exchange.

## 10. We Have Lost Capacity for Form

We don't build community because we've become informal – impatient with what we dismiss as mere formalities, and incompetent to create form, which we dismiss as empty and so not worth learning to make well. Whereas G. K. Chesterton said "Free men always create institutions," we've largely accepted that making them ourselves is silly and pointless. We've developed a dualistic sense that man-made institutions are worldly and not worth our effort, while the Church is God-made and so is set apart from our efforts, ideas, skills, interests and affiliations. That dualism results from and perpetuates the 'torn social fabric,' or 'missing middle,' where our collaborations should be creating structures that weave the world back together, provide erosion control, and offer rich interface between the Church and the culture, the Kingdom and the world, Christ and perishing humanity.

**Do It Anyway!**

In short, we don't build community because we're bent, busy, broken, flattened, scared, misinformed, weak, lazy, distracted, worldly, and sinful. Actually, God has chosen such weak things to undermine the powerful, fools to humble the wise, and the small to confound the great. You're it! You and your fellow Christians, together, are the hobbits, the fellowship of friends, the companionship of the Way, by means of whom Christ is to be mediated to the rest of humanity.

'Together' is the key word. Wherever two or more of you gather in His name, Christ is in your midst. With even one other person, you have a 'form' – this friendship, this marriage, this book study, this conversation – a form, with the supernatural potential of being filled with the presence of Christ. It has the externality of a boundary, or definition, of 'self', and the interiority of capacity for welcome. As you experience being present to Christ in the gaze of another person, you awaken to Love in a new way.

Light shines from such vessels-of-unity in a way that opens to other persons. Christ can be more and more present in the world as His Body is more and more fully knit together in true community. He feeds us in Eucharistic communion and sends us out not to face the world alone, but to realize that communion, that Christ-in-us, in the shared life of community.

So, we have the formula: two or more, with Christ in the midst. The form you two or ten create can be just for you or open to others; of long or short duration; cheap or expensive; purposeful or purposefully aimless. Your time together gives new meaning to the word Incarnation. If Christ is embodied within these lived experiences of togetherness, each one is a fresh encounter with Him for each of you and for those you welcome. Just the awareness that relationship can be three dimensional – can be *place* for encounter with Christ, can be form, can be structure-that-welcomes – changes mere connection into community building.

**Failing Forward**

The stumbling block in building community is form, or *means*. God chose to be communicated by means of imperfect, natural forms such as persons, words, works of art, ritual and gestures. When the perfect Word asks to be uttered through us, we cannot wait to become perfect before we express Him. We are made – as individuals and as a community – in the tension and discomfort of communicating Him, of becoming virtuous, of learning to be community, even if badly.[4] The forms 'person' and 'Church' are not man-made works of finish-able perfection, but man-and-God-made works of growing perfection. What is good, true, and perfect coalesces over

---

[4] "A thing worth doing is worth doing badly." G.K. Chesterton

time into more and more stable form. What is bent, broken and imperfect is shaken and tested over time to reveal and heal structural weakness.

We are to be people of the Word, but must become, ourselves, better forms. We might also become more skilled in the creation of such forms in order to contribute our small excellence and holiness to the building up of the whole Church-as-communicator-of-Christ. We know the Holy Spirit has protected the doctrines of the Church from error. Let us set aside, for the moment, questions about whether the Church's own authorities are adequately protecting the liturgical forms, spaces, and signs given into their care.[5] That leaves, for laymen to focus on, the responsibility for improving in virtue, in communicative power, and in capacity to receive meaning from within forms. We must understand that virtue, that power, and that capacity to involve us in the good of the whole Body of Christ. Just as there is no development of structure unless flour is kneaded into a form, there is no such thing as the single believer rising up free and powerful without communital structure, the work it entails, and the dimensionality it makes possible.

The community you inhabit cannot be a perfect form, because it is a working-into-structure of all the imperfect forms within it. Like the family, it is a messy form filled with becoming. Unlike the family, it has been given, supernaturally, all the means necessary for its

---

[5] Of course you care about these forms, argue about these forms, and have valuable contributions to make to protecting and promoting these forms! I only ask you to leave them aside while we consider you, as a form, and the possibility that you and your forms also communicate Christ to the world.

fulfillment. There are perfections within the Church that have crystallized over time and through hard work, and perfections infused into her form as pure gift. The family is the 'domestic church,' or small fractal of the larger whole, but it is not sufficient unto itself. Just as the individual person is a *locus* of Christ, but must have the external support of the Church, the family needs the Church as its context for becoming.

We cannot turn from the work of community to circle the wagons of isolated families or individuals without undermining the mission of communicating Christ. We cannot ignore the need for virtue – power to be good and power to be good at communication – without undermining the mission of communicating Christ. We cannot leave 'communicating Christ' to professionals, experts, artists, or people who seem good at it without losing the life-blood that must be kept coursing through the Body of Christ to keep it strong and healthy. Certainly, the further reach of the Word into the world depends upon the core strength of the Body of Christ to be, and to be good at being, community.

Here are five principles for building community, and then I'll give some practical tips and ideas:

## 1. Context Over Content

The context of relationship – persons knit together in unity; fellowship raised up as a vessel of encounter – is more important than the content. The game you play, the food you help cook, the art you make, the book you read, the language you practice – all are secondary to the community you strengthen by sharing these aspects of life together.

*2. Semi-Permeable Boundaries*

Structure-less, boundary-less, too-open forms dissipate or implode. Too closed, narrow, impermeable forms collapse. The one can't bear the weight of the actuality of persons – their flaws, conflicts, needs and struggles – and the other can't bear the weight of their glory.

*3. Interior Freedom and Unity*

The capacity for the presence of persons must be cultivated and practiced. This is not 'us working on our relationship', but 'you working on yourself' – learning to recover interior freedom every time you lose it. Interior freedom is to the individual what unity is for the married couple, and to the Body of Christ: space within structure, form open to the flow of love. You need to learn not just to work with, tolerate, or hang out with others, but to open yourself to let them in, to affect you, and to be loved by you. It's the practice of humility, communication, courtesy, reciprocity and unity, for all of which community is the necessary training ground.

*4. Perseverance in Difficulty*

Impedance and interference with the forward momentum of a project are part of the adventure. The delights of ease in relationships, feeling fully known, sharing interests and creativity, knowing you belong to the other and are loved, being thrilled together by the success of your project – these are qualities draping the form you create together with blood, sweat, and tears.

*5. Leisure: Secret of Fruitfulness*

People who play together stay together. We can be creative alone, but we need each other for the play of generativity.

"Creativity is bringing into the world a new thing, new perspective, new life, new hope; harrowing hell, bringing light into darkness, turning walls into doorways, resolving tension and yielding to the play of God upon the Self as instrument. The further possibility of generativity is that the forms we create might become vessels in which Christ is communicated to others."[6] The capacity for freedom, for being at leisure with oneself and others, for creativity and for generative play begins in holy leisure – deep restedness whose origin is Christ in the Eucharist.

## Practical Suggestions

### Be Interested, Invested, Involved

Communicate your desire to teach, to meet, to study, to help. Communicate your need. Leah Libresco, responding to Rod Dreher's ideas in *The Benedict Option*, asked her friends to offer whatever resources they had to share.[7] They realized that sharing needs was also a great gift, opening the door to community-building reciprocity. Communicate your constraints: I have First Mondays open from 10-12; I can only meet once, or in alternate months; I need to ask for $45 for each lesson; I'm handicapped so I need someone to drive me; I'm scared of building community so I want to start with a one-time, no-ongoing-commitment, public-place get-together. Often 'spiritual' people become dismissive of their own 'non-spiritual' interests, skills and desires. Instead, cultivate those together. Personal

---

[6] Charlotte Ostermann, *Souls at Play – Reflections on Creativity and Culture*

[7] Rod Dreher, *The Benedict Option*; Leah Libresco, *Building the Benedict Option*

particularities lend themselves to robust inter-connection with others. It's a mistake to think of 'holy' as 'smooth,' less personal, distinct, or 'craggy'. Be a 'stickleburr,' (not a BB!) investing in and inviting others to share your interests.

Any wholesome thing people do together is a good thing for Catholics to do together. Catholics might pray together before hang gliding, read *Caritas in Veritate* together instead of *Principles of Macro-Economics*, offer to *teach* weaker chess players instead of just crushing them, or invest in cultural initiatives instead of stocks. Or, they might not. There's no requirement that your intentional relationships and activities have a Catholic stamp, Catholic or even 'spiritual' content, or a service aspect. You are Catholic, so the context (you two-or-more) is Catholic.

*Be a 'We'*

Once you have a 'we' – even just one other person – articulate who you are and what you want to do together: Catholics playing chess monthly; close friends meeting weekly to discuss struggles with eating disorders; old geezers offering Saturday morning home and auto repair help to young whippersnappers, people learning French at Tuesday brown-bag lunches for conversation practice; etc…; etc….

*Extend the 'We-ness' to Others*

Now decide how open this fellowship can be to others, without becoming something you won't enjoy. You may already have several 'community seeds' going that can be defined more carefully so as to open them to others. You may decide to keep it private and not admit others, but to pray together for an intention beyond your own interests, so as not to become closed in upon yourselves. How can our 'we' embrace others, without violating our own selves or the reality of that 'we'?

*Be Small*

Schedule for those who are committed, no matter how few, and then open to others if you've not reached the limit of your openness. Don't chase after a mutual time from more than a handful of people. I was once so disappointed when a book study was cancelled because only I and one other showed up for it. The facilitator wanted to wait until more people got on board, so it never happened, and I missed being woven together in love with those two persons through conversation about that book.

*Evaluate and Iterate*

G. K. Chesterton said "A thing worth doing is worth doing badly." Try something! Wobble, fail, evaluate what happened, restore the unity, and make adjustments to the design as you go. Over-planning for perfection has been the death of too many initiatives. Disembodied abstraction prevents realization of the idea of community. One advantage of being together is that we have each other's support in the disappointments and failures. Working through them together is what knits us together. Our unity is the context for Christ's presence in our midst, and it grows stronger by such exercise. Failure is rich in information that can improve your future self and the future of your friendships. Friendship itself can be an 'emptied sign' – superficial alliance unrooted in deeper meaning and community – or a beautiful form full of deep unity, purpose and welcome for others. Evaluate your friendships to see possibilities for positive change in those microcosms of community.

*Be a Convener*

For several years as a speaker for the Catholic Homeschool Conference, I passed out an invitation to conversation. "Gather some friends, choose a book or topic, invite me over to give a brief presentation, and then let's talk!" One person finally asked, "Do you really mean this?" Since I did really mean it, she gathered some friends and coffee, and we've had some great hours of conversation over various books and ideas. I'm just the Conversation Starter, and we go on for 3 or 4 hours from my initial presentation. A good conversation takes time and a good, juicy topic. That topic need not be lofty and spiritual. Among Catholic people, all things lead to the One Thing. I've had animated conversations about Frankenstein, neurology, economics and regenerative farming, for instance. And don't get me started on fractals, complexity and network theory! Reality has an appeal for Catholics, as our Faith is rooted in affirmation of reality.

*Be a Connector*

Sometimes you can serve the cause of building community just by connecting people you think might be interested in knowing one another. I connected a young Catholic film maker to a friend with a film project, an artist to a contest opportunity, a potential donor to a start-up project, and an iconographer to potential commissions. Friends have connected me to publishing and speaking opportunities, or directly to their kids with the opportunity to teach. It's interesting that the vocations of Teacher and Artist can only be fully realized in community. The Church has not fully realized its responsibility for the artists in its midst, or for the cultivation of persons through poiesis and creativity

– perhaps because in the weakening of community is the demise of the Gift economy to which artists correspond, and perhaps because the Church is, like a person, continuing to grow up.

*Say Yes.*

I want to say yes to whatever comes my way, because I believe God places treasures in my path for the taking. Of course there are times I must say no, but you'd be surprised how much I've been able to say yes in true freedom. Each one of those commitments of time, energy, and resources has been a learning experience, has given me back more than I put in, has been a win-win for me and someone else, has been part of the great adventure of life. A friend called once and asked if I'd be game to make donuts together. We both had a copy of a cookbook with Edna Ruth Byler's Potato Dough recipe, and neither of us had ever ventured to try it. "Yes!" I said, and a few days later we were schlepping excess donuts around to friends together. Edna Ruth's recipe made 200 donuts and our two families couldn't absorb them. Twenty years later we were still hosting a Mardi Gras party – frying up 800 donuts by then for that annual feast. I'm glad I said yes!

Much community building is just "the care and feeding of friends," or "the art of friendship". What are you interested in doing with your fellow Catholics? What would you try if they wanted to try with you? What would you do if only you didn't have to do it alone? What dream of yours needs the cooperation and participation of others? My son puts on a summer play with a small group of theater-type friends. I used to have choir buddies who would break into *Gaudeamus Igitur* at the restaurant where we had a few beers after rehearsal. I'm pretty sure we were our waitress's favorite customers!

My daughter Hannah and her friend Lucy held weekly tea parties at the campus center. They simply committed to one another, and it would have been delightful for just the two of them to come. It wasn't long before college students joined them for scones, the staff found the party and showed up, and my future son-in-law was introduced to the girl of his dreams. Tours for incoming students and their parents on Friday afternoons eventually included a stop by the lively tea party for a glimpse of the center's attractive community life. Hannah notes: "If tea parties had been restricted to those both of us could show up for, they would not have flourished. So even if it takes two to generate and institution, it may only take one to maintain it, with the influx of new life – like a baby!"

We've had medieval dinners with friends – complete with stale bread trenchers and a dragon piñata for the boys to slay with their wooden swords. Is it 'building community' if you mummify a chicken with friends, or make Montessori materials together, or ask for help pressure canning vegetables? Yes! If it's life and you share it, if it's interesting and you pursue it, if it needs to be done and you do it with friends, then it's building community and, thus, building the Church. Is there a story you'd like to bring to life, an exhibit you need help to create, a trip you'd like to take, a language you'd like to practice, a book you'd like to read, or a chore you need help with?

Look for ideas from others. I'm amazed by the organization behind *Diner en Blanc*. Flash mobs of couples elegantly dressed in white bring their own tables and chairs, dinners, white tablecloths, cutlery, flowers and stemware to a public space to dine *en masse* without explanation or speeches. The mob disperses on cue, with no further interaction until next year's *Diner* is scheduled via word-of-mouth and internet channels. Priya Parker introduced me to the idea of the Jeffersonian Dinner.[8] A carefully curated selection of guests dines together and shares answers to provocative questions posed by the host/hostess before the event. One person at a time speaks and then after table discussion of his thoughts, the baton passes to another. Parker has found that the more structure provided for an event, the more guests enjoy it. Nobody is worried that others are expecting something they don't know about, or can't give. As Chesterton says, it's the clear boundary of the fence that makes a great playground.

*Healing the Wounded Body*

There's a deep wound in the Church which presents us with a new opportunity to invest ourselves in healing the very Body of our Lord. Natural, local, organic, unconscious, parish-style community used to thrive by necessity wherever people were thrust together geographically – for better or for worse. This is the sort of community celebrated in the novels of Wendell Berry – the loss of which he evokes with poignant beauty. It's not likely we'll recover the kind of community that results from being stuck with each other. Mobility and speed and technology have rent that fabric – perhaps beyond repair – leaving us with an opportunity to practice interior freedom in the face of a daunting array of choices about how we spend our time. Deep community bonds are formed from sharing real life, together, as much as you can. The new opportunity is to invest in conscious, intentional community building within the constraints of your real life and limits, freely.

---

[8] See: Priya Parker, *The Art of Gathering*

As scar tissue criss-crosses a wound to provide scaffolding for regrowth of healthy tissue, our networks of affiliation – based on interests, faith, professions, needs – can help heal the wound where community should be. Is intentional, "man-made" connection as good as that old-fashioned, natural connection? Well, it's different…in some ways less satisfying and effective, but in some ways better. When you hear the word 'networking,' you may think 'schmoozing for business advantage,' or 'superficial connection.' But it's entirely possible to 'network' with altruistic and generous intentions, and to deepen your network of association into some authentic friendships, creative collaborations and generative institutions.

A robust, resilient network results from multiple, overlapping interconnections among its 'nodes,' or centers of contact. Some of us are more widely connected than others, but every relationship strengthens the overall matrix of support for deeper healing.

Like freedom, community can be 'real,' while becoming 'real-er,' as we aim for the fullness of its eternal 'real-est-ness'. To speak of failure in building community is not to speak ill of the reality, but to aim to realize it more and more fully as the Kingdom comes. The more we are 'we,' the more we can act together in love so that the watching world sees the miracle of Love uniting disparate people together in Himself – in Love. The Holy Spirit moves back and forth in the Body to reweave, illumine and animate it so that Christ may be communicated not as an abstract concept or ethical system, but realized as a community of love.

The Church is not a collection of individuals who became Christians and then got together for potlucks. It is the collection of persons drawn together by Christ, who were made a people by witnessing His resurrection and receiving into themselves the Holy Spirit, who gives coherence to His Body over time and space. The people He called His own recognized themselves to be the *ecclesia,* nurtured by Mother Mary, whose task was to proclaim the lived reality of His victory over the grave and His continuing, Eucharistic Presence among them.[9]

---

[9] See: Luigi Giussani, *Why the Church?*

Chapter 2

# Persons are Form, Rising

From the vast, overarching mystery of God to the deep, impenetrable mystery of the human person, there must be a *Way* of reconciliation. From the divinity of Christ to the humanity of His people, there must be a *path* of integration and, thus, freedom. From the lowliness of sinful man to his divination, there must be a *means* of transformation. That Way, that path, that means is the human person. By God's own design, man fully realized is where the Word at the origin of all being – *imago Dei* – meets the Form of its fulfillment – person. The Church, as the Bride of Christ, is the person-form generated of man-material to receive and signify participation in the life and love of the Trinity.

We participate as forms in the 'middlework' of communicating Christ, or mediating His presence. We are tiny seed-like structures, perfectly placed to communicate Him, as the Word (our *logos*, law, or spiritual DNA) resounds from within each unique, unrepeatable 'cell' in His Body. By the practice of words, of communication, we grow into structures that resonate with the Word at our origin. Our conversations about literature, science, social justice, history, economics, education, art, and such prepare us to engage with, learn from, affirm, and practice articulating ideas that expand our reach into the culture. His Church, as it is knit together in community life, can and should practice the loving unity, civility in disagreement, dialogue within and between circles of affiliation, active listening, and interested conversation, which all prepare a people to turn further outward, together.

The Church, as Christ, as a membership, and as individual believers, communicates Christ to the world. To the extent we fail as communicators, we fail at this primary task.

To the extent we individuals of the Word become a community – a Body with one head in full communion with Christ; a person with the integrated wholeness of mind, heart and body that conveys Truth, Beauty and Goodness in the freedom of Love – to that extent we may, as Christ-in-His-Church, communicate Christ.

To the extent we are, individually, people of the Word, growing in virtue – powerfully in-formed by correspondence to Truth, and out-formed by power in expression of truths – we can become more effective communicators and collaborators in reaching the world for Christ.

The work we do to become people of word strengthens the Church to voice Christ's response to the realities He encounters through us. As a Body, as a community of love, we grow ready to face the increasingly difficult communications between the Church, the 'aliens' in the midst of the growing Kingdom, and the often hostile world. As we collaborate to bridge gaps, create new forms, reweave the torn social fabric, dialogue and argue with error, we will be becoming 'people of word' – interested in and practicing skill at word use.

The magnitude of the task should not daunt us. Only when we recognize that it is impossible do we acknowledge it must first be God's work. In our smallness, we can but participate. Yet it is exactly *through* the smallness of one person, one family, one friendship, one form that God has chosen to do the work of communicating Himself. Where do we begin? Where the person begins: in the womb, in the home, in the Church. These are forms connected analogically, and illuminative of one another as a result. Their relationship suggests we look toward the education and formation of persons in capacity to receive and to express Christ, or to *real*-ize Reality. We can look at the project of 'becoming a *people of the word"* as community-building, and, on a smaller scale, as a process of individual formation and education.

To so proclaim the Good News in and through our lives that we weave an atmosphere of hope within which fellow believers and non-Christians may find shelter and encounter Christ, we need more than certainty of Catholic doctrine, important as that is. People of the Word need persuasive and argumentative power, emotional depth to couch truth in love, artistic skills of many kinds, capacity for generating social institutions based on transcendent values, and a lot of practice in the arts of conversation, teaching, and interpersonal communication.

The classical education model suggests a helpful framework for education that moves organically from Gymnasium (movement and music in immersive context) to Grammar (play and practice with building blocks), to Dialectic (the *logos* of tension and struggle), to Rhetoric (the science of self-expression), to Poetics (participation in the art of making new things). As a Catholic response to the classical framework, I suggest that we adjust its linear perspective to account for our continuous development of capacity to receive and give new forms in every stage, even as we age, linearly. A more 'three-dimensional' model lets us start where we are to develop along each of these trajectories at once, simultaneously, through a full spectrum of possibilities, instead of walking along a line with a narrow, chronological focus.

To communicate Christ, we need to speak the language of form and freedom freely, in every possible form.

**The Language of Form**

The 'grammar stage' in classical education is the point of departure for studying any subject. It involves learning to think in words – forming and being formed by structure and meaning in communicable *means*. Because Christ's goal for us is 'glorious freedom,' we may readily take it that freedom is the goal of words; is the quality, or state, brought about and supported by excellent verbal structures. Because Truth is that-which-sets-men-free, these structures must in some way participate in Truth to have the power to accomplish their highest end.

The 'truth' of a form has to do with its content (Is the message true or false? Is this painting a forgery? Does the data support the conclusions of this author?), its excellence, or virtue (Is the story well written? Was the experiment designed well enough to test the hypothesis? Is this the craftsmanship of a master builder?), the fit between material and message (Was a singing telegram the best way to give the news her brother had died? Would unleavened bread be better for the Eucharist? Would 'citizen,' or 'resident' be the better word to describe him?), the successful integration of its components (Did the musical score support or detract from the film? Is her character as beautiful as her face? Does the modernist altar do justice to the medieval cathedral?), how well it conforms to an ideal form (Is this book consistent with Catholic doctrine? Was this truth conveyed in a loving way? Did the soufflé rise perfectly?), and similar considerations.

The starting point for studying communication is 'word,' but that word, itself, does not quite convey the fullness of meaning in the phrase "In the beginning was the Word." Naturally, our words are subsets, or derivatives, of The Word, but if communication-of-Christ is the essence of word, then other means-of-communicating-Christ must also, analogically, be 'word.' Indeed, every created being, every person, every free act, every man-made thing may also proclaim Him, and so is 'word' in its way.

The word I have chosen, to include more of what is meant, is 'form'. Others speak of Form (capital 'F') as the invisible Idea behind all material things, or of form (lower case 'f') as merely-material things. Form (Fform?), here, means that which in space-time has the potential to communicate that which cannot be contained within space-time. Words, or forms, are means by which meaning is communicated, between persons, across times and places, and by which transcendence is woven into the fabric of the social and material world. It can be frustrating to hear the words 'form,' 'word,' 'person,' 'act,' 'artwork,' 'creature,' 'content,' and 'context' used so interchangeably, but the language of form is poetic, multi-layered, and metaphoric by design. It actually corresponds to reality in its connectedness to the matrix of Holy Wisdom, and thus allows us greater access *to* reality.

**Person as Form**

The human person is, neurologically, made of words – informed by the structures of language, disposed to engage the world through the mediation of words, and not fully realized until he expresses himself in word, act, created form. A German child does not learn German 'naturally'. He has a natural inclination to respond to language, but if he were left to his own devices in a German-free world, it would not emerge from within him. Language is a gift from the people around him that corresponds to that natural inclination – itself a supernatural gift. He does not 'learn' German so much as ingest it. Little verbal structures cloaked in relationship awaken his hunger for language. As he appropriates words, their relationships – to persons, to things, and to one another – generate a network of neural structure. Like a placenta, this verbal-neural, physical-emotional, intellectual-visceral, actual-imaginal, internal-external interface mediates the world to him, and him to the world. Reality – vast, and incommensurable with his smallness – and Person – vast, and incommensurable with the smallness of space-time – are woven together in correspondence through en-worded experience.

The rich, immersive, loving environment which is the best for language development mirrors the natural world – rich with forms communicating about their Creator, and mirrors the Church – rich with art, music, architecture, rite and ritual, verbal structure, drama, and relationship. All these forms invite persons into the work of becoming, and into the adventure of discovering their correspondence with reality. The forms are enormous, complex, intimidating, forbidding, and hard to enter into – veiling the meaning they carry so that by working through the veil, we children develop the capacity to receive all they offer. The forms around us both attract and repel, invite and deny entrance, veil and reveal. By means of them we develop capacity for all reality – *capax omnium* – that characterizes 'persons' as the highest forms of all.[10] We begin *in context* – forms we didn't create are the scaffolding for our becoming.[11] Just as reason begins in reasonable trust, persons begin *in* person-supporting forms.[12] Thus forms-as-content develop into forms-as-contexts which pressure those inside toward the meaning, values, norms, language, and possibilities that those forms are trying to convey. Truth in form invites the freedom of those it touches. We'll dig deeper into the dynamics of that process later in this chapter.

The human being is form which communicates (not merely telling about, but actually transmitting that which is beyond the scope of his material being to generate) the image of God, or the Word at the origin of his being. Simply, any form is a carrier of both intended meaning and the person of its creator, to whomever receives that form. Forms have more, or less, capacity to transmit 'meaning from beyond' (beyond the page, beyond this moment, beyond the literal message, beyond time), depending on their goodness, truthfulness, and beauty. Their integrity and the integrity of large structures made of smaller forms is a function of how well and how far these transcendent values are knitted together in them. They are *sound* when they resonate with truth, *good* when they effectively accomplish their purpose, and *beautiful* when they hint at the glory of the Lord. Forms have, because all Creation has, a Trinitarian

---

[10] James Schall, *Docilitas* pg. 160: "The human mind…is *capax omnium*, a capacity or power to know all things. This means primarily knowing the relation of things one to another."
[11] Fr. Giussani: "The I begins in the encounter with reality."
[12] Per *Fides et Ratio*, reasonable trust is the basis for reason.

structure that corresponds, at small scale, to the Father, Son and Holy Spirit. We'll get into that in more detail in Chapter 8 – The Arts of Communication.

**Form is a Doorway to Reality**

The Trinity is the origin of form. Christ is the ultimate form of the Trinity. Creation and all further forms lead to the matrix of Holy Wisdom through, or because of, that 'triangular' structure that seems to be the fingerprint of God. The 'triangle' that describes the process by which Reality becomes Form through Persons also describes Christ becoming Church through Eucharist, and Seed becoming Fruit through Tree. We will see that, because form leads outside itself to its creator, it becomes a doorway to the possibility of freedom, or an invitation to freedom. Form both gives and denies access to the realities and meaning it embodies, or carries. Material resists being shaped into form, and the skill of the creator often loses the battle for perfection in form. Thus, form 'veils' its meaning to some extent, but is necessary for communicating it. Even God's creations veil, in their smallness, simplicity, ugliness, or location, His glory. Each one is a communication to us from our Creator, but we must learn to see *through* them to marvel at the artistry of the Love who made them. Even a burned meal can convey the love of an inexperienced cook to her new spouse, for instance. Even the symbolic communion that represents the Sacrament of the Eucharist has power to draw people to Christ.

**Persons of the Word**

Reality, as known in a Person, is re-presented in him to be communicated in form. The form reduces the reality it represents to a more accessible proportion, and invites us into encounter with that reality through metaphorical or material means. Through the form both the reality and the person who makes the form may be encountered. For example, a territory is mapped by an explorer or cartographer, whose map gives travelers better access to the reality of that place. The map maker himself has a style, a way of investing careful hours in its production, and thus is also knowable, to some extent, through his work – the form of the map. Through a poem, we encounter both the reality experienced by the poet, and the poet himself. A scientist might help a student understand the immune system by using the metaphor of war – and convey his own awe and passion in the enthusiasm of his teaching. We might examine a plant or animal for information about that form, and also be drawn to contemplate its Creator through wondering at its intricacies and beauty. We may know a person well, and through reading his stories, or examining his drawings learn about him in greater depth.

There is skill to be learned in order to appropriate what is given in form. I need mathematical fluency to enter into a form such as a statistical data base. I need to speak French in order to read literature in that language. I need to have some life experience and understanding of what it means for a writer to be true to art in order to read Flannery O'Connor's novels well. I need a prerequisite course before I may enter the advanced class. He who *has* (skill, interest, sensory acuity, trustworthy guides, wonder, intellectual faculties, docility, infrastructure, imagination, etc…) is able to appropriate more from form. The rich grow richer, and those who *have not* may lose capacity to hold form at all.

Verbal skills lead to intellectual development, and power to make verbal structures (encyclicals, plays, thank-you notes, speeches, textbooks, etc., etc…) with truth, beauty, goodness, power, coherence, and excellence. To become *'capax verbum'* – to have capacity for the Word – involves something more than skill, however. People of the Word must be indwelt by the living Word, nourished by His actual Presence, growing up unto Him in every aspect of being, aiming to be perfect as He is perfect.

We are in the world, but not of the world. The material of persons is, to some extent, word. We cooperate with the making of ourselves as we interact with the multi-layered realities that enclose us. Because those realities are portals beyond the world, this interaction builds us up of stuff from beyond the world. Each form generates more of such form – opens in us into a scaffolding, or infrastructure, that supports the appropriation of reality, or – if it is a lie – generates a stronghold that closes in upon us by de-forming us for correspondence to reality. Correspondence to reality generates our freedom, and issues forth in the affirmation of reality which is at the root of worship[13].

To some extent, we are all deformed – by original sin, by the violation of our purity, by the untruth in even the best forms around us, by the lies we've believed – and we are all supplied with the image of God, which is Reality calling us toward Himself. Each person-form is a portal to the reality of God, or can be said to have this longing for God (what

---

[13] See Josef Pieper's *In Tune with the World: A Theory of Festivity* for more on the roots of worship in the affirmation of reality.

Fr. Giussani calls 'the religious sense') at his core.[14] When that longing is met by the Word, Christ, willing to come directly into us to dwell, we receive the new organizing principle that structures us for correspondence to Truth, the new opening principle that enlightens our previously darkened minds, and the seed of Christ-life that bears fruit in the realization of true newness of life. The Way He provides for this becoming-fruitful, or moving toward our destiny, or working out our salvation, is the process of appropriating and making form.

To communicate Christ, we first appropriate and then re-present Him. Simple, but not easy!

**The Dynamics of Freedom**

You, fully realized in freedom, powered by love, radiating glory by means of your unique, unrepeatable particularity, are a form your Creator is making, with your co-operation.[15] Only the highest, most amazing material – *person* – could be a self-conscious co-operator, a free actor, a realizer and responder to all that is real, or a bearer of the image of God. The work you do to become virtuous, to develop skills with particular media, and to communicate is co-operation in the work of a Master Artist to make You. By the practice of communion, community-building, and communication, you co-operate in His work of making His Bride, the Church. By collaboration with other members of His Body, you co-operate in the incorporation of all humanity into His Kingdom, the realization of all Creation, and the unique, unrepeatable fulfillment of the form that is You.

---

[14] Luigi Giussani, *The Religious Sense*
[15] Ephesians 2:10 – "You are God's **workmanship** (*poema*)…"

The simplicity of the repeated pattern that generates and perfects form (in our case, the pattern "appropriate and communicate Christ") issues forth in a powerful dynamic – back-and-forth movement that echoes, or participates in, the movement of the Spirit. As Love moves back-and-forth between Ideal and Actuality, Form rises in the chiasm, or center of that going and coming. The movement is not circular, or pointless, but spiral – continuously centered upon and rising within the full realization of the I-Am-Fulfilled-in-Christ. Man is 'the point' of the movement of Creation, because Christ rises as man, by way of Man. The Church, as the context of that rising, is, likewise, centered upon the human person fulfilled in the glorious freedom of Christ. She rises up in history, despite waves of structural crumbling and renewal, as the Bride. Love has moved, is moving, and someday will perfectly have moved through her to invite all men into His Kingdom where, in her womb, *person* is, once again, 'the point'.

Returning to the personal scale, the first and most important, foundational dimension in this dynamic is you, becoming free, cultivating capacity for appropriation and expression of the Word in Love. This involves all your physical, emotional, intellectual and spiritual capacities. It begins before birth and becomes more and more intentional and focused as you grow up. Though you are, at all points in time, 'three-dimensional,' you move more and more into the second-dimension of self-realization as you practice communication-through-form. The 'second dimension,' then, is the growing self-awareness, self-expression and self-direction that makes possible the formation of community. I call this your 'metaphoric dimension,' because it proceeds by means of metaphor. Your self-awareness (and, often, Scripture) places you in juxtaposition with other forms (Mom and Dad, siblings, trees, pets, buildings, pottery, stars, etc…). By means of likeness to and differentiation from them, you grow in knowledge of Self.

**Form Develops Dimension and Gravitas**

Form rises to become 'structure'. Structure, as we have seen, is a mixture of truth and error, wheat and weeds, perfection and bentness, sound-amplifying and sound-deadening form. Structure is compounded of forms that lend it their qualities. Structure might overcome, or might amplify the qualities of the forms it is made of. What is certain is that those qualities *matter*. Literally, the qualities of form materialize, for good or ill, in the qualities and integrity of structures. Each structure, then, is a new form with greater-or-lesser structural strength and greater-or-lesser capacity to communicate, truly and well, what was in the smaller forms of which it is made.

As forms rise to 'three-dimensionality' they rise into structures with the quality of 'interiority'.[16] A fully realized form, or structure, has a boundary-of-self and an interior-within-which an Other may encounter both the meaning expressed and the person of the communicator. This two-way-ness of form is what makes it a center of two-way, vertical-and-horizontal, natural-and-supernatural communication. Like the Cross, each form (each person) has both a material *gravitas* that draws like a magnet, and a radiant power that draws like a beacon of light.

---

[16] A fascinating look at fractals and the possibility of a dimension 'rising' between 2- and 3-dimensionality can be found in the film *Fractals: Hunting the Hidden Dimension*, a PBS Nova documentary.

That such Meaning as Christ could descend into such form is, in itself, a miracle. He first raised up a people of law, gave them interior correspondence to eternity through the practice of Sabbath, and then purified a Woman to be the receptive vessel of the new Adam. All our works, acts, and forms begin in the receptivity to Christ exampled in Mary's *fiat*. The Church is the context of the possibility of personhood, as Mary is the context of the Liberator of persons. All our forms are derivative of the Word at our origin – the Form at the Origin of all Being. The indwelling structure of the Trinity points the way toward the restoration of persons in Christ, and that way leads through us, through the Church, and through Mary to the Word who dwells richly in us.

The two-way-ness of forms makes them 'mediating structures' that communicate what-is-inside, out, and what-is-outside, in. Man is participating in the fulfillment of Reality by appropriating, discovering, knowing, understanding, affirming and stewarding all that *is*, and returning it to God in worship. So, you (and God's other works of art) and your forms (words, acts, creations, gestures, institutions, artworks and other responses to reality) are participants in God's own work of communicating Himself. You have boundary, exteriority, particularity, accidents, and limits, which both veil and invite through the veil. You have *capax omnium*, interiority, universality, essence and eternal being, which issue forth in light, power, sound, meaning, and beauty. It may seem strange that, though the imperfections of that exterior-facing Self muddy communication, they also make it possible. It may seem odd that the intangible radiance of a form can be a forbidding force that seems to repel, even as it invites to entrance.

Each form is a 'center,' defining by its small boundary a universe of 'not-this-form,' and including, by its correspondence to reality, that whole universe as 'not-yet-realized'. Each of your forms is something of a communication from you, and from your Creator as well. Beauty can and does 'knock you for a loop,' and in the face of it you may feel your other-ness, outside-ness, and unbeautiful-ness with painful acuity. Brokenness and ugliness have a certain attraction for those who are wounded, deformed, and small. Understanding this paradox of form helps you learn to communicate Christ with love for those who receive your forms. Love helps to resolve the tension form may create in those who receive it. Love helps to cultivate capacity for form in those who receive it. Your freedom allows for the free flow of love into and through your forms, as each free act expands your freedom.

The measure of the integrity of form is freedom – the degree to which love (or message) moves through it effectively. The quality that allows light to move freely through a window is 'transparency,' or 'translucence'. The quality that prevents electricity from moving freely through a wire is 'resistance,' or 'impedance'. A person whose physical movements are free has the quality of 'ease,' or 'grace'. That full-of-grace quality is familiar to us as the supernaturally protected purity of Mary, or the graciousness of a hostess who puts all her guests at ease. Verbal structures have integrity when they bear up under scrutiny and analysis, support act that corresponds to reality, and have clarity, or are free of obfuscation and manipulation.

To the extent you are free, you have the fullest possible capacity for Christ, and thus the greatest possible power that you, as form, can have, to communicate Him. To the extent your two-way structure and the structure of the forms you create 'correspond to reality'[17], to truth, they will be gravitational magnets drawing others toward Truth, radiant lights showing the Way of Truth, and structures-within-which Truth resounds, is amplified, and calls every other form into a kind of 'judgement' as to whether it resonates with Truth.[18]

If the matrix of Holy Wisdom is the infinite correspondence between the persons of the Trinity, then all Creation and all derivative form can be said to be built upon, or to be in some degree of correspondence with that substantial-but-non-material form – creating word spoken into a context of perfect correspondence with Love – which thus corresponds to Reality in all its manifestations. The freedom of the artist is transmitted in, or as, the Truth carried in his works. Each form becomes an invitation to freedom to the extent of its Truth and the extent to which it is given in the full freedom of its maker. We'll look deeper into that process of formation, which corresponds to the dynamics of freedom, in Chapter 8.

You cannot control how well you, or your forms, accomplish God's purposes. Only see to their integrity and to your freedom as much as you can, and leave the impossible rest to Him.

Consideration of form, and the dynamics by which form becomes communicative structures and contexts for formation in truth, acts as a ladder of proportion, or relationship, by means of which we may move freely between the lowest and highest forms in order to learn

---

[17] Luigi Giussani: "Freedom is the correspondence to reality, in the totality of its factors."
[18] See Elaine Scarry's *On Beauty and Being Just*

about ourselves and about the process of communicating Christ. The 'form' at the chiastic center of all this form-making and form-realizing action is 'word' – the Word who is a Person. The flights of contemplation and the hard-as-concrete work of actually making communicable forms begins and ends in 'words,' however insufficient that form seems for the task of being the Alpha and Omega, the origin and destiny of all Creation, the image of the is-and-was-and-ever-shall-be-creating God.

**Persons are Words, Rising**

To move up and down on the ladder of proportion analogically is to move from one form to another by means of their similarity, their relationship to other forms, their correspondences to one another. Metaphor is the means by which we think from one thing to another. We can only approach God analogically, but He has given every created form to show us something of Himself. He desires to be known, and to be the model for our Catholic theory of communication.

Words are the means God works with to raise up persons. Not only your mind, but also your emotions, will and spirit are build up by the action of words. For example, life changed profoundly for blind and deaf Helen Keller when she was finally given words in a form that developed her capacity to think and communicate and respond to reality in words.[19] Mankind has grown up, since the Fall, in his use of reason, as human beings increased in word power, and

---

[19] See Keller's autobiography, *The Story of My Life*. A more recent autobiography, Ghost Boy, by Martin Pistorius, offers another fascinating example of a person brought to life and woven back together by words.

power to use the language of mathematics that underlies the material world. Man grows either infantile as he loses the power of *logos* (logic, word), or insane as his words lose touch with truth. The Church, also like a person, has grown up as she has lived out the Word deposited within her and ordered her doctrines and teachings more and more into words that could communicate Truth clearly to the world.

**A Simple Summary**

Because Christ the Word is the 'content' at the origin of all being, we can say He is like a seed of light opening outward from within us as infrastructure, or life-support scaffolding that encourages us to grow and become fully realized. Because He is the context of all becoming, we can say Word is external structure made communicable to nourish our growth. Because Word is the fulfillment of all being, we can say Word communicates Love that calls beings toward their destiny. In the case of human beings, that destiny is to be raised into the community of the Trinity, where we will live eternally in that perfect Love. We can further expect to have the world of created forms restored to us as the New Heavens and New Earth, where we may discover each form fulfilled as a vessel of Love's communication of Himself.

If words were food, we'd have to eat and digest them. If words were air, we'd have to inhale and exhale constantly so the bronchioles in our lungs could have as much contact as possible with oxygen. If words were light, we'd need to just bask in those rays to absorb them. If they were seeds, we'd want to plant them in rich soil so they could open and grow. They *are* like all these things, so we do well to be in their presence, take them in, *and* encourage them to grow.

So…we have a goal: overflowing with words of life and light; and a means: words….What is the method, the way to get the most from words? Christ is the light inside waiting to open up, and Christ is the Truth outside waiting to be taken in. Why are we not surprised that Christ is also the *way* – the action, or movement, or method by which this will be accomplished? He asks to be taken in, He asks to be lived out…and that's the way. To use an almost ridiculously simple image, the method could be expressed this way: Grow a bigger sponge, immerse it in words, and squeeze.

We grow in capacity for words by working with them, using them, improving them. If we enjoy words, go to Mass, live with those who use words, or seek to learn anything about the world in all its variety, we will find ourselves willingly immersed in words. The squeeze comes when teachers require a paper, when a friend asks us for the reasoning behind our beliefs, when a eulogy or sermon is needed in our community, or when we discipline ourselves to write an article or blog post about what we've learned. Making that form is the making of us. Grow, Immerse, Squeeze, Repeat.

There's one form that seems a perfect context for growing, immersing, and squeezing sponges, and that is conversation. Josef Pieper calls conversation 'the context of truth,' as it is such a central place for the development of human alignment with truth. So, we'll turn to conversation in the next chapter, to communication science and word-work in Chapter 4, and then to dialogue as a vessel for the living Presence of Christ in Chapter 5.

Chapter 3

# Conversation – Context for Truth

"We need artful conversation. Cooperation is its operative principle, enthusiasm its divine breath, and its power to raise spirits is supernatural."[20] Conversation is a form which develops in the midst of us. Each one is as unique as the persons and the particular combination of persons who make it. Of all the ways to immerse oneself in words – reading, journaling, collecting words, browsing a dictionary or thesaurus, memorizing poetry and Scripture, doing word art, playing word games, writing stories, etc.... Conversation is arguably the most fun. Like any game, it grows more exhilarating as the skill of the players increases. Like any form, it has boundary, substantiality, actuality, concrete limitations, and pointy particularity. Also like other forms, conversation has an interior dimension, and the foaming-into-form structure of any substance infused with something of a different order. One must be a participant and not merely an observer to experience it. The living quality and beauty of a conversation still touch your heart as long as the form lasts in memory.

Unlike some other forms, conversation is ephemeral – rising up and then fading away, almost as a wave forms to approach the shore, then disappears. Those waves carry so much material so effortlessly and, hopefully, so often, that surprisingly substantial form develops from the bits

---
[20] *The Art of Conversation,* Catherine Blythe, Gotham Books, NYNY 2009, pg. 17

of words and phrases and ideas that cohere in participants' minds over time as supportive infrastructure. Thus does the context of conversation become a powerful means for the conveyance of content from person to person. This life-to-life transfer is the lifeblood of education, or formation of persons. Fr. Schall tells us "truth ultimately exists in conversation. It needs to come alive when someone is actually knowing, speaking and hearing it. That is when it is luminous precisely as truth."[21]

In *Reclaiming Conversation*, Sherry Turkle says "conversation is on the path toward the experience of intimacy, community, and communion."[22] Conversation (*con* = with + *versatio* = turning) is a turning back and forth together, within which a message may be conveyed without resistance, or even amplified by the intimacy and support of loving relationship. Conversation without this quality of love and trust is likely to end, to become non-form, quickly. "Conversation implies something kinetic. It is…about the activity of relationship, one's 'manner of conducting oneself in the world or in society; behavior, mode or course of life.' To converse, you don't just have to perform turn taking, you have to listen to someone else, to read their body, their voice, their tone, and their silences."[23] Conversation can have the qualities of a journey, a symphony, a campfire, a river, a bridge, a feast, improvisational comedy, jazz music, a romp in the waves, or (as Peter Kreeft has said) a "bubble harness" for the

---

[21] *Docilitas,* James V. Schall, S.J., St. Augustine's Press, South Bend, Indiana, 2016, pg. 143
[22] *Reclaiming Conversation – The Power of Talk in a Digital Age*, Sherry Turkle, Penguin Press, NY, 2015, pg. 7
[23] *Reclaiming Conversation – The Power of Talk in a Digital Age*, Sherry Turkle, Penguin Press, NY, 2015, pg. 45

living form of light-in-words that bubbles up in this context to be held in caring human presence.[24]

The context of conversation pressures, or influences those within it toward coherence and unity. These people, these topics, somehow 'go together' and find a way of fitting in to this whole form we are making. Because it blooms into the space between persons, conversation offers a taste of, or a living metaphor for, the experience of Christ-in-the-midst of His two or more.[25] Here, in the acoustic space we generate together, the word dwells richly as it bounces among us, gathering to itself the material of our reading and experience, the power of our passion, and the association with those we love and trust.

A conversation is an intimate, limited, space-time infused with the all-of-reality and the promise of eternity that loom large outside our little we-ness, here-ness, and now-ness. Conversation can be the Golden Mean that proportions what is vast or too-large downward, in love, to accommodate an Other who is small-in-capacity and otherwise could not bear the weight alone. In this aspect, conversation partakes of the love and humility of the art of teaching, and gives opportunity for its practice. Conversation is practice, also, for the presence of persons. Within this context – usually, first, among family and friends – we learn patience, courtesy and unity that lay a groundwork for more public civility as we grow.

---

[24] *If Einstein Had Been a Surfer: A Surfer, a Scientist, and a Philosopher Discuss a "Universal Wave Theory" or "Theory of Everything"*, Peter Kreeft, pg. 39

[25] Matthew 18:20: "For where two or three are gathered together in My name, I am there in the midst of them."

Here, because we love, we are motivated to speak in love. Needless to say, this gets harder as the distance – emotional, spiritual, cultural, ideological – grows between persons. We need the practice! If we're going to become 'people of word,' we also need practice thinking out loud, putting thought into words, telling stories, listening, taking turns, respecting others' opinions, and seeing to it everyone gets a chance to be heard. We need conversation in order to become good at the play of ideas. Conversation allows the same kind of play with words and ideas (small, interlocking, multi-use building blocks that form amazing structures) that keeps kids with Legos™ absorbed for hours of creative fun.[26]

**Content is the Infrastructure for Conversation**

Those building blocks are the forms your conversations are made of – the topics and ideas, stories, maxims, jokes, testimonies and questions that are logs on your conversational bonfire. The more truth and power there is in the components, the greater the strength and integrity of the larger structure – conversation – and its power as a context to order participants well. Conversation, like every form, should align with Truth in order to be a context of formation toward Truth. Truth, in this context, is not only the factual truth of whatever is said, but also the upholding-within-the-context of truths taught by the Church, such as the goodness of edifying one another, the badness of gossip or impurity, the need for cultivation of charity for each other, and the positive value of thinking (together, aloud) about things that are good. "…whatsoever things are true,

---

[26] See Charlotte Ostermann, *Upschooling*, Chapter 9, "B is for Brick" for more on "building with bricks".

whatsoever things are honest, whatsoever things are just, whatsoever things are pure, whatsoever things are lovely, whatsoever things are of good report; if there be any virtue, and if there be any praise, think on these things."[27]

Truth-in-conversation also involves the integrity of the form itself. Though there is no single 'ideal,' it's clear we want to aim for a lively, enjoyable, provocative interaction with contributions from as many participants as possible, and with great goodwill among them – shown as courtesy, interest in and engagement with one another's ideas, and whetting of the appetite for the eternal community life we all anticipate. If it can also educate, strengthen faith, help us practice our verbal skills, and bond us together in temporal *communio*, so much the better.[28] Truth-in-conversation may also mean a truthful and charitable discussion of error, sin, lies, or evil. Such content can and should be included and handled in light of the maturity of participants, with care to emphasize the counterpoints of the Faith, and to minimize unnecessary specifics of the content of evil.[29]

There's plenty of content available for participants of all ages, so let's turn to what you may have to contribute to the conversations you help create.

---

[27] Philippians 4:8: "Finally, brethren, whatever things are true, whatever things are noble, whatever things are just, whatever things are pure, whatever things are lovely, whatever things are of good report, if there is any virtue and if there is anything praiseworthy—meditate on these things."
[28] See: Hans Urs von Balthasar, "Communio: A Program" in Communio International Catholic Review, Vol. 33.1
[29] Ephesians 5:12: "For it is shameful even to speak of those things which are done by them in secret."

**Have Fun with Words**

Put a dictionary, a thesaurus, and/or an etymology dictionary on the table and dig for whatever looks interesting to share and spark conversation. As in the popular game Balderdash, but with no score-keeping, take turns guessing the meaning or roots of an obscure word. Let one word lead to another, to far-flung associations with life and literature, or to impromptu poetry. Conversation is a great place to model and share the love and enjoyment of words for their own sake. Words are delightful in themselves, and not only valuable for their function.

**Ask Opening Questions**

Find out what books you all have in common, what places you've all been, what authors have been key influencers among you. (Any of these may be the springboard for a long conversation, or help recharge it midstream.) What have you just finished reading? Did anyone learn anything interesting this week? What topic could you talk about for hours (here, just give us a quick peek)? Who is the strangest person you've ever met? What's your favorite movie (be careful not to derail the conversation into a movie plot unless everyone is really interested)? What would you do if you won a million dollars? What non-profits do you support, if you don't mind sharing? How are you like your parents? Different? What questions do you want answered when you get to Heaven?

## Ask for Stories

Open the floor for quick, real life stories (and be patient with those who aren't yet good story tellers...this is where they learn). Ask for funny, family, injury, adventure or misadventure, conversion, scary, bad boss, neighbor conflict, embarrassment, failure, success, pet, travel, or other specific story categories, or leave it to participants (categories really help people find stories in memory, and help draw them out by giving a sort of permission). Among the 'regulars,' there will always be repetition of stories already heard, and this is one of the perfections of conversation. We are meant to hear one another's stories over and over within close community. Repetitive orality is at the root of all written literature. Don't groan as the story begins, but enjoy it *because* you anticipate the details, the familiar expressions of the storyteller and his enjoyment of the sharing, and the music of the human voice given scope to play out loud.

## Catechesis and Proclamation

Formal catechesis is a special kind of teaching, perhaps best reserved for the form 'class.' But conversation is a wonderful form for mention of the doctrines with which we are all meant to become 'conversant'. "...the context within which the transmission of the Faith flourished was that of friendship," say the authors of *The Craft of Catechesis*.[30] The more you learn about the Faith, the more, naturally, will be on the tip of your tongue to work into conversation

---

[30] *The Catechism of the Catholic Church, and the Craft of Catechesis*, Pierre de Cointet, Barbara Morgan, Petroc Willey, Ignatius Press, San Francisco, 2008 pg.13

naturally, without turning a living conversation into a dead vehicle for an assertion. If those doctrines don't have anything to do with the living of your real life, you've got problems bigger than creating a great conversation. If you've all been to the same sermon, or read the same article or book about the Faith, those are easy topics for little-way catechesis. "…the etymology of 'catechesis'…is derived from the Greek word 'catchein,' originally meaning 'to echo' …Catechesis, then, is the 'echoing' or 'resounding' of a message."[31] *Resound* something that inspired you. Your response to that lived experience will carry the message with the power of life-to-life transfer.

Your own testimony of transformation of lives (your own, and others'), answered prayer, or your real experiences offering apologetics for the Faith and answers to real questions about it have a place in conversation. These have the power of story form, which helps carry them to others. Just remember that those others are fellow participants and not your audience, congregation, or students. Many kids have never once heard their parents tell a story about how faith has changed, or helped, or rescued, or challenged them. This sharing of faith life has more power than formal catechesis to influence others toward lived relationship with Christ.

Speculation about the New Heavens and New Earth is a great topic of conversation that generates an atmosphere of hope, in addition to building one another up in excited anticipation of this very real future. In a delightfully non-morbid way, it also helps prepare everyone for the

---

[31] *The Catechism of the Catholic Church, and the Craft of Catechesis*, Pierre de Cointet, Barbara Morgan, Petroc Willey, Ignatius Press, San Francisco, 2008 pg. 63

inevitable deaths of loved ones we all experience.[32] Eucharistic miracles, miracles of healing, and miracles hoped for all contribute positively to conversations and strengthen faith.[33]

**Object Lessons**

> "St. Francis did not only listen for the angels, but also listened to the birds."[34]

Every God-created form is full of potential to attract our interest, give us cause to be amazed and wonder, show us a glimpse of His glory, fill us with questions, and provide analogic access to His mind and qualities. Creation is full of material for sharing in conversation. You'll have to learn to adjust the 'formal lesson by lecture' style to a more rapid-fire conversational offering, but do share whatever has caused you to wonder and contemplate.

You've got to follow your own interest, placing your mind "into the essence" of whatever attracts you, but here are a few topics with intrinsic 'object lesson power': Electricity/step-down transformers (How can that priest reach up to receive whatever power it takes to turn a wafer of bread into the living Christ?), water (Life could not exist without its three-form structure!), bones (How does internal structure set you free?), the heart (Where are the two-way, listening and balancing the whole body, pulsing

---

[32] See: Fr. Charles Arminjon, *The End of the Present World and the Mysteries of the Future Life*
[33] See: Joan Caroll Cruz, *Mysteries, Marvels and Miracles in the Lives of the Saints*
[34] *St. Thomas Aquinas*, G.K. Chesterton, pg. 29

and pausing, sending and renewing lifeblood structures in the Church?), placenta (The Church is a mediating structure!), the promised land (Why might you find your enemies gigantic if your faith is small?), trees ("We shall be like trees…" [35]), lungs (I thought they were empty!), foam (Now I'm seeing it everywhere!).

Whatever you learn and share with passion transmits both facts that may be forgotten, and wonder that is contagious and becomes part of the persons with whom it is shared in living conversation. Facts can be exchanged even between machines, but wonder and passion communicate through personal presence.

**Error**

Let's say that there are three levels of dealing with error: as material for discussion, for a dialogue, and for argument. Here, we'll discuss error as a topic for conversation among family and friends. Probably, the persons involved in the conversation are not party to the error, or, if they are, they are loved and relationship between you is an important part of your life outside this conversation. Further on, we'll discuss dialogue, persuasion and argument as somewhat more emotionally distant kinds of conversations, with 'proponents of error,' or 'opponents of truth' present to engage with you in different ways. In Chapter 5, you'll work with the Other to find as much common ground as possible, and identify the territory of disagreement with civility and interest in the relationship. In Chapter 6, you'll consider the best means to teach, or persuade an Other toward the truth – inviting him to higher ground. In Chapter 7, you'll work against the Other, in a sense, for his sake and for the sake of truth, to correct and lead him toward truth.

---
[35] Psalm 1

Ultimately, the relationship may fail if it is threatened by your telling of the truth. It may fail, unnecessarily, if your telling of the truth lacks skill or love.

One of my favorite sayings is "Truth can comprehend error, but error cannot comprehend truth." I believe G.K. Chesterton is the source. If it was someone else, I can't find it in my notes.[36] At any rate, it sums up an important dynamic in the handling of error. If you're the one standing in the light of truth, you can see all around the error of the Other, but that person cannot understand your position well. This means it is incumbent upon you to make a path for him to move from his position to yours. It's not enough, in conversation (especially with children listening in), to say that Position "X" is Wrong. You need to be able to show where it went wrong, where it's 'off' from 'true,' or skewed. If you don't understand how people got into a wrong position, you won't be of help getting them (or those drawn to their position) out of trouble.

If the proponent of an erroneous proposition is not present, you must try to present their ideas with truth and fairness. St. Thomas Aquinas, for example, made it his business to articulate clearly the heresies he then refuted. By demonstrating understanding of the longing, or need, or honest reasoning that might lead someone onto the path of error, you are modeling love for your 'enemies' and showing you can find what is good and true even within those who disagree with you. This is critical modeling for your children, as they will need to voice disagreement with you whenever your proposals of truth do not seem to correspond to their lived experience. They must see you can handle it without vilifying them, and that the fear you feel

---

[36] I did discover in Fr. Schall's *Docilitas*, this related thought: "It was Aristotle, I believe, who remarked that virtue can know vice, but vice does not know virtue." *Docilitas*, pg. 126

when they express agreement with error is overcome by love. The person is more important than the position, and that's true even when they are not present to a conversation about their beliefs. Charity in the absence of persons is the best assurance there will be charity when they arrive.

Charity can help you have compassion for, and understanding of the reasons people end up mired in unbelief and lies. They are wounded, broken, needy. They've been raised without faith, in families without fathers, by mothers who have hardened hearts due to their own mistreatment, in schools with hostility toward faith and family, and by media (news and entertainment) that provides lies as content within contexts built of lies. They have a deep religious sense, or longing for the love that can only be found in God, but have misdirected that longing to fill the aching need with money, sex, drugs, food, entertainment, distraction. They have believed a lie and it has turned into a magnetic black hole, attracting 'proof' that the lie is true. That proof has become a prison, or stronghold against the truth that would free the prisoner. They are in bondage, are de-formed, are very little able to receive and appropriate truth (as someone starving loses capacity to take in food), and are hard put to believe in reality or objective truth.

Just remember that conversation is a great place to examine and challenge erroneous notions, if you can hold love in your heart for the actual persons who are trapped in those abstract ideas. Love should lead to sadness. Fr. Giussani taught that sadness, not chirpy hopefulness, is the opposite of despair. If you do, indeed, hold out hope for the victims of lies, then you will feel sadness at their current plight. Despair lets you cut them off without your own heart being wounded.

## The Impact of Impediments

"The impeded stream is the one that sings." (Wendell Berry)

Since conversation is a group effort, it will be affected by the skill, maturity, personality, experience and interests of all participants. It's amazing that with so many factors that could all clash and contribute to the failure of conversations, so many do so very well! Some topics are too divisive and others are lead balloons, but good conversationalists can usually keep the ball in play despite defects in content. The context of player quality matters more for the shape of the conversation within. Here are a few of the players you may encounter:

The Multi-Tasker – Nods and smiles, but keeps moving his attention away from the conversation – usually back to his cellphone. If he's trying to work, read a book, or watch a movie, the conversation is probably an unwelcome intrusion, best moved elsewhere. If he's having trouble choosing between virtual and actual life, don't make it worse by trying to drag him back into sync here, now, in reality. That enables him to feel he can juggle both. Just act as though he has chosen to exclude himself, because he has.

The People Person – Welcomes everyone passing by into a conversation. This generous impulse can end up derailing the conversation with every new entrance. Model, or suggest, welcoming people in with a wave or nod that, itself, models non-disruption. At a break in the flow, you might bring a newbie up to speed quickly (to keep up the flow of that topic), or stop and make introductions as a transition to a new topic.

The Finisher – Has trouble listening to slow sentences and may rush the speaker by finishing them to speed things up.

Even if his fill-in-the-blank is correct, it's rude. Granted the frustration of listening to someone who does not form his thought in words before holding the floor by uttering a few, one simply must not supply words for another unless asked.

The Contradictor – Any bold assertion or authoritative tone without the backing of experts provokes him to flat contradiction. It may stem from a habitual approach to conversation as competition, self-defense against being influenced by others, or a feeling that his own thoughts are negated by contrary ones. If the speaker can take it in stride, without escalation of defensive reactions, that's for the best. Other participants can modulate the combative tone by expressing interest in hearing, or charity in championing alternative positions.

The Solver, or Fixer – An open question is posed and he gives the Right Answer in a way that seems to shut down any other response. A difficulty is mentioned and he has The Solution, and no interest in other approaches. Someone mentions a personal flaw, or weakness (to be understood, to be real, to give context for his perspective) and The Fixer dives in with a program of action. He doesn't realize this was not a request for a fix, but an offering of Self meant, merely, to be received and accepted in love. You might suggest, "Let's get some other answers on the table so we can compare them," or "Let's brainstorm for several possible solutions before we focus on any one approach." In the uncomfortable pause while a person shrinks from being fixed, offer a look or touch that shows solidarity, some flaw of your own with the admonition that comments are not welcome, or disarming humor if you have that knack.

The Lecturer – Holds the floor too long, doesn't notice the subtle clues that others are antsy to move on. He probably hasn't had much practice with pithiness in words, or the passing-the-ball teamwork that makes for better conversation. He seems to be talking 'at,' rather than 'with' you. He may interpret your questions-that-show-interest or your questions-that-lead-elsewhere as competition, so show love as you reach for the ball.

The Inner Ringer[37] – Finds one or two in the group with whom to exchange specialist content (We three can recite every word from that scene in that movie. The two of us could talk all night about the failure of that book to follow the conventions of detective fiction.). They don't notice everyone else courteously not speaking since they can't contribute. Unless they peel away, or the group re-forms to exclude them, nobody else can participate. Either way, they've damaged the original form in the having of their own way. If they move into a contra-conversation to avoid boredom with the current speaker, they make more tension for those trying hard to listen with love, and may undermine the confidence of one who is new at practicing conversational skill. There can be a subtle superiority involved, which Inner Ringers enjoy.

The Positivist – Cannot seem to endure hearing anything he considers 'negative', and tries to shut down such lines of thought with a 'high moral ground' tone. We can gently prevent gossip, detraction, etc… without undue sensitivity preventing such topics and hyperboles as "The Gullibility of the General Public," "What is Not Going Well at Our Church," "Why I Disagree with That Bishop," or "People Who Say Nuke-u-ler and Ree-la-tor Should be Shot!" One has only to read C.S. Lewis's *That Hideous Strength* to resist forever the deadly pull of "nice-ness".

---

[37] C.S. Lewis, "The Inner Ring"

The Clueless – Completely oblivious to the subtle clues of others trying to indicate things like "Please speak more quietly in this restaurant," "Careful – everyone here isn't Christian," "I'm uncomfortable with this topic," "I have zero interest or expertise in that topic," "Someone here is having trouble getting a word in," "Keep your focus on the speaker, please, even if he's stumbling," "I'm also interested in others besides you," "I really need to get home," etc.… They actually may not pick up on the hints, or they may have an interior demand that if someone won't speak up, they don't deserve to be heard. On the other hand, The Wordless can also be refusing to use verbal structure to bridge tension, and have an interior demand that others pick up on their subtle clues.

The Withholder – Makes no contribution, even of "I am an interested listener" signals that encourage others to continue. Charles Derber, in *The Pursuit of Attention*, after studying thousands of face-to-face conversations, offered three forms for such "support response":

- Background Acknowledgements: Minimal acknowledgments that you're listening, such as "Yeah," "Uh-huh," "Sure"

- Supportive Assertions: Acknowledgments that show active listening, such as "That's great," "You should go for it," "That's not right"

- Supportive Questions: Questions that show interest in hearing more, such as "Why did you feel that way?" "What was his response when you said that?" "What are you going to do now?"[38]

---

[38] *The Pursuit of Attention: Power and Ego in Everyday Life*, Charles Derber

The Hopeless – Discusses how bad things are (and we do need to talk about that) without affirming reasons for hope. No conversation should be a temptation to despair, and the light of the Kingdom shines ever brighter in contrast with whatever is dark. To edify, or build up, our fellows in conversation, let's not go down into dark rabbit holes without also helping everyone up and out. Much-needed criticism (of policies, practices, laws, positions, etc…), likewise, should be a call for the creativity of persons in community, in an organization, in civil society – not an end in itself.

**Tension in the Room**

Conversation is a physical, aural, mental unity of persons in tension. Even to give attention to another is to tense toward him (as may be shown in leaning toward him, looking interested, being a bouncy and responsive 'surface' for reflection of his words) and away from noises and side-conversations around you. To look at a speaker while also caring for (and noticing and responding to) the others is to be tensed in two or more directions at once. To have words uttered by another suggest in you a connection, memory, or new idea that must wait (and, yes, you might forget it… aaaghh!) puts you into tension.

To be bored by, or impatient with, but yet to love another is interior tension for you. To hear mis-pronounced words, split infinitives, or mixed metaphors is agony for some. To hear inane speech that seems disconnected from thought, meaning, or purpose may feel unbearable. Barbed wit, quick topic-hopping, literary allusions and other specialist references, invented words, puns, the sparks from iron sharpening iron[39], voices raised in passion and enthusiasm, fingers pointed or tables slapped for emphasis, are for some the highest delights of conversation well played and, for others, trigger fear or insecurity. It would seem to suggest that conversation is a game you just can't win. It's actually a game we can only win together.

Only Love, flowing through your freedom and among you all in the context of unity you create together, can bear all this tension. And this is the glory of conversation – that Love does bear it, and resolves the tensions in new-to-every-conversation ways. These impediments all help the stream sing, so don't let the possibility of discomfort keep you from the fun of conversation. Skills help, practice helps, spiritual growth helps. A good leader, host, or facilitator and good rules help, which we'll look at in the next chapter.

The first rule, the ultimate skill, and the essential art of facilitation is Courtesy. It is first, because, like love, it undergirds all other rules of engagement. It is highest, because it corresponds to the context of love that best characterizes and makes possible all conversation. And it is essential for the host or leader who stands *for* Love in the tension between and among the participants in a conversation – by loving them all.

**Courtesy Resolves Tension Creatively**

Courtesy is considered by many to be mere formality, form emptied of meaning, or false structure imposed upon authentic life to undermine it. Stratford Caldecott disagreed:

---

[39] Proverbs 27:17: "As iron sharpens iron, so one man sharpens another."

> The elemental courtesies of conventional etiquette and good manners are the vital channels for preserving this spirit in everyday life. …an education that actively cultivates such modes of behavior will begin the process of building a society that is liturgical to its very core, in which the 'air' of grace can circulate. Harmony of soul can only be restored through effort, and the restoration of manners and kindness is an important beginning. Without it, little else is possible.[40]

He was speaking of liturgical renewal, and we should highlight the connection between conversation, courtesy and liturgy to further emphasize the importance of all three. For those who consider liturgy to be mere formality, form emptied of meaning, and false structure imposed upon authentic worship, the answer is often to abandon, dismantle, belittle, and endlessly change the Form with, apparently, no awareness of why it was there in the first place. With G.K. Chesterton, I caution you never to remove a form before you thoroughly understand its purpose, and without a very clear idea toward which re-form is moving.[41] Even imperfect forms have value and serve to hold up

---

[40] Stratford Caldecott, *Beauty for Truth's Sake*, Brazos Press, 2009, pg. 130

[41] G.K. Chesterton: "In the matter of reforming things, as distinct from deforming them, there is one plain and simple principle; a principle which will probably be called a paradox. There exists in such a case a certain institution or law; let us say, for the sake of simplicity, a fence or gate erected across a road. The more modern type of reformer goes gaily up to it and says, "I don't see the use of this; let us clear it away." To which the more intelligent type of reformer will do well to answer: "If you don't see the use of it, I certainly won't let you clear it away. Go away and think. Then, when you can come back and tell me that you do see the use of it, I may allow you to destroy it."

structures or accomplish purposes in ways that may not be readily apparent to those who perceive the form as old, broken, unnecessary, irredeemable, ridiculous, or otherwise empty. "We need to learn some manners."[42] Margaret Shepherd agrees:

> In addition to listening well, the other simple principles of civilized conversation – don't ramble, don't gossip, don't bore, and disagree carefully – are not arbitrary demands of etiquette; rather, they are based on caring about yourself and about others. Etiquette and manners are not out-of-date rules. Instead, they are generally accepted guidelines for making everyone comfortable enough to connect.[43]

Stephen Carter, in *Civility*, in which he offers some rules for the more public conversations you will have in the civic sphere, finds the roots of civility in the small forms that make up civilization:

> Erasmus popularized the concept of *civilité*.... *Civilité* is often translated as *politeness*, but it means something more. It suggests an approach to life, a way of carrying one's self and of relating to others – in short, living in a way that is civilized. The ideal arose 'at a time when chivalrous society and the unity of the Catholic Church were disintegrating,' so that Europeans were casting about for guidance on how to avoid killing each other. The word *civilité* shares with the words *civilized* and *civilization* (and the word *city*, for that matter) a common etymology...meaning 'member of the household.'[44]

---

[42] *The Art of a Lively Conversation*, Alain de Botton, Utne, March-April 2009, pg. 52
[43] *The Art of Civilized Conversation*, Margaret Shepherd, Sharon Hogan, Broadway Books, NJ, 2005, pg. 3
[44] *Civility*, Stephen L. Carter, Basic Books, NY, 1998, pg. 15

You might say that rules of courtesy, instead of being empty forms, are forms that carry the meaning of loving one another into compounds of the household, or *oikos* in which family members love naturally. Thus, form (words, gesture, act) allows the natural, concrete forms of our togetherness to cohere where love is more a matter of choice and civil behavior than feeling. If we simply dismantle the form (as opposed to spoofing its emptiness hilariously as a reminder it must be filled or die hollow)[45], an anarchic, rule-less, unsafe and unloving sort of society results, which we cannot easily call 'civilized'.

The answer, then, to empty form, is to refill it. Let your courtesies be filled with love, be rooted in love, be forms that convey love to others, and they will never become false cover for hatred of your fellow man.

---

[45] See Oscar Wilde's *The Importance of Being Earnest*, anything by P.G. Wodehouse, and Oliver Goldsmith's *She Stoops to Conquer*, for examples.

Chapter 4

# Communication Science in Light of Christ

I have said that I hope this book will contribute to a Catholic theory of communication. I prefer the word 'science,' (from *scientia* = wisdom) as it encompasses theory and practice. But 'Communication Science' has become an academic discipline, set apart from this project to some degree, as experts often are from Everyman. I want to draw upon the enormous body of work that represents communication science without smothering this book's aspirations to inform lay Catholics and communities.

Communication professionals fill all sorts of roles in marketing, public relations, knowledge management, human resources, education, etc.... They are one and all of enormous help to the Church as she communicates her various messages to the world. Ultimately, though, our Catholic, person-centered, 'wisdom' of communication is for those in-dwelt by the Word Himself, and only touches upon this science tangentially.

To communicate Christ is the mission of every Christian. Freely, He gave himself to us, and so, freely, we give Him to others. It sounds easy, but in practice we encounter roadblocks and impediments to the flow of Gift. Modern communication science helps illuminate the difficulties, but is insufficient to the task of communicating a living Person. The Church has learned much, and continues to learn, from various secular communication models and theories, while developing her own practices and theology after the pattern of Christ. In this section, we'll look at communication theory, a developing theology of communication, and the 'middlework' by which we become communicators of Christ, even if not communication professionals. The goal of this book is:

To improve the 'core communication strength' of the Body of Christ so as to improve the Church's effectiveness, or 'extension strength,' in communicating Christ to those outside the Church.

It is my hope you will grow in awareness of the task, the skills, the forms, and the collaboration that can make our shared mission a shared adventure.

## The Context and Content of Middlework

Christ is the Word. He wants to be communicated, but communication is more than the transfer of information. The world doesn't need more information about Him. The world needs the actuality of Christ, given through the actuality of His Body, the Church. The world needs to know that He is present now – available, teaching and responding, living and acting in His Church. We must communicate better internally, in order to keep the Body healthy. We must grow better able to communicate Truth in new forms, and in diverse cultures. We must become an active, listening presence in the world so that the response of Christ to the realities we face may be voiced.

The possibility of communion of persons must be lived, through Christ, in real sharing of life and ideas if it is to show up against the cultural background of parodies and illusions of 'community'. Christ chose to locate himself, and we can do no less. He is in the world, and His kingdom is emerging *through* the Church. Our ability to engage in common activity and conversation, and even to struggle through conflict to real communication and resolution, depends on the reality that this communion with others is possible. Within the Church we are to live a life of communion with Christ and His Body which shows the world the true end, or value of human community.

The mission is not merely to speak true words about Truth, but also to become a *context* – a person, a people – within which the Word himself may dwell richly, and resound. A free, integrated person is an integrating context, able to welcome others into encounter with Christ.

## Communication – Theory, Theology, Practice

*Communication Theory is Helpful*

To better understand yourself as a "communicator of Christ," it helps to think of the human person as a form created by God expressly for this purpose. Your *being* proclaims him, as you bear His image into the world, whether or not you actively share the Good News. Just as you create forms – words, gestures, acts – to communicate, so God created you, and the Church. Original sin deformed man. The image of God, or 'message' he carried became darkened, or lost in noisy interference. Christ, the perfect and ever-sounding 'signal' returned to man the capacity to resonate with Truth, with Himself. Not only are you changed by the indwelling Christ – into a 'new thing' that re-sounds the Word – but the entire 'communication environment' changed with the coming of Christ. Christ's presence makes possible the 'transmission' and 'reception' of the gift of faith. "Thanks to the Redemption, the 'communicative capacity' of believers is healed and renewed. The encounter with Christ makes them new creatures, and...introduces them into the intimate life of the Trinity, which is continuous and circular communication of perfect and infinite love among the Father, the Son and the Holy Spirit."[46]

Communication theories consider the way a message is encoded into form, transmitted, and then decoded by a recipient. "Success" depends on many variables, and is achieved to the extent a message arrives intact and is accurately understood, or perceived. Early theories had a somewhat mechanistic feel: if we send a clear message in unambiguous form (the words "I love you," for example, instead of flowers) without impedance (face-to-face, for example, instead of through a potentially garbled telegram), the message will be received successfully.

Later developments in communications theory placed more emphasis on the interpersonal nature of the exchange. Do the sender and receiver speak the same language, have a common frame of reference, share the metaphors and life experiences that make up the form of the message? Is the emotional, or psychological receptivity and/or intellectual capacity of the recipient conducive to successful reception of the message? Are there messages in the environment that cloak, or conflict with, the message being sent (such as facial expression and tone of voice, a noisy or frightening setting, or a communications technology that introduces interference, or seems impersonal)?

---

[46] *The Rapid Development*, 6

Concerned with the effectiveness of message-sending, communications science seeks to account for and optimize as many of the variables involved in communications as possible. The more whole-ly the communications 'environment' – social, emotional, cultural, physical, historical, intellectual – is understood, the more complex becomes what at first seemed to be simple human exchanges of information. Developments in neurology have expanded our awareness that we process auditory and visual data quite differently; possess cognitive filters that treat messages differently based on their alignment with memories or preconceptions; have significant message-blocking responses to perceived danger in the environment or in the message itself. Further complicating the 'simple' process of communicating a clear message is the explosion of the number of communication channels – electronic technologies, social media, advertisement on every surface – each with their own contributions to make to, and ways of interfering with, effective communication.

Clearly, the task of communication is beyond symbolic, beyond technical, and beyond comprehension and control. (Sadly, it is not beyond manipulation, which we will explore further on.) It cannot be the case that, in order to communicate Christ you must have an advanced degree in Communications Science, Educational Psychology, or Media Studies – helpful as those disciplines may be. A "theology of communications" begins where theories meet the reality that communication is beyond the reach of abstraction and analysis. In fact, our best 'science' has revealed how amazing it is that communication – complex, nuanced, multi-variant, and beset with obstacles – ever occurs!

## A Communication Theology is Developing

Dr. Christine Mugridge and Sr. Marie Gannon have done a masterful job of documenting the development of a true Theology of Communication. In *John Paul II Development of a Theology of Communication*, the authors survey the response of the Church to the growing understanding of the complexities of excellent communication. Through *Inter Mirifica, Evangelii Nuntiandi, The Rapid Development*, World Communications Day addresses and other encyclicals and documents, they trace the Church's work of knitting together secular communication and media theory with the implications of the Incarnation. Finally, Pope John Paul II's *Ecclesia in America* is shown to demonstrate "a working theology of communication," with communion as its highest purpose. "Defining the parameters of this theology is the prerogative of the Church. Understanding this theology and applying it is the responsibility of the Catholic/Christian Communicator."[47]

Through the Church – the lived communion of man with the Trinity – we offer communion to the whole of humanity. A Catholic communications strategy begins in encounter with the living Jesus Christ and transforms the Church through the transformation of each member – awakening desire to share His living presence by an excellence in communication activities that is modeled upon His own example. This theological awareness serves as a foundation for the incorporation of communications science principles and methods into the communications strategies of all Church entities (parishes, dioceses, seminaries, media outlets, etc…). The authors demonstrate

---

[47] Dr. Christine Mugridge and Sr. Marie Gannon, *John Paul II Development of a Theology of Communication*, pg. 24

that the communications theology modeled in *Ecclesia in America* developed in continuity with the existing patrimony of the Church.

> According to John Paul II, the means of social communications must become a way of communicating the fullness of the truth of man as revealed in Christ, for this is the only authentic foundation for solidarity and the realization of the integral development of all humanity according to the divinely ordained potential and dignity of the human person.[48]

**Communication's Return to Persons**

Theology returns us, then, to the human person – the communicant who receives Christ, and the communicator who shares Him. The form 'person' manages the impossible task of transmitting Person in form, Self in form, message and meaning in form. That the Word of God is at the origin of all form – all *being* – is the foundation of a theology of communication. That all word moves toward fulfillment through Christ-in-His-Body, in an *exitus-reditus*, or back-and-forth movement of Love, generates an overarching context for human communication centered upon the fulfillment of human personhood in communion with the Trinity. In this context, the 'form' carries the message 'Christ'. The context has the quality of 'love'. The person in the center of the Spirit's movement is realized as he utters truth in love. The communication of Christ is the making of the person (and thus the Church) who communicates Him.

---

[48] Dr. Mugridge, in an interview by Carrie Gress: https://www.ewtn.com/catholicism/library/john-paul-iis-theology-of-communication-6051

The communicating person may be relatively passive – simply *being*, held in being by Love, nourished by the Eucharist, radiant with the image of God that he *is*. Or, he may be relatively active – moved to utterance by the Word who dwells richly within him, growing in the skills of word-use and verbal sword-play, collaborating to create new and more effective forms of expression. What is key to the effectiveness of the Christian communicator is the life and growth of Christ within him. The language of presence transforms a potentially abstract science and remote-from-life theology into a person-centered practice of self-donation that mediates God to the world through Christ, through Church, and through individual Christians.

The message "Christ" is 'successful' when it sets persons free, and is draped in the quality "Love" when it flows freely through a free person. Since, as Fr. Giussani has said, this freedom in a person is the degree to which he corresponds "to reality in the totality of its factors," his capacity to speak truth in love is a capacity to voice Christ's response to the reality he encounters. "…the Person of Jesus Christ reveals and establishes the three communicative principles or moral imperatives of the overriding importance of freedom and truth, respect for the dignity of the human person and the promotion of the common good."[49]

As Christ is communicated, the person of the communicator grows in freedom. What freedom is to the individual, unity is to the Body. "…the essential nature of the communication of the faith is that it produces the unity that perpetuates it, and equally interesting, as the faith is communicated it grows and is strengthened. …

---

[49] Dr. Christine Mugridge and Sr. Marie Gannon, *John Paul II Development of a Theology of Communication*, pg. 55

unity within the Body of Christ is maintained by the language of Presence."[50] Our lived unity, or community, within the Church is the basis of our solidarity with those in the world who need the Church to be an active listening presence, as well as the voice of Christ's love. "The renewal of the Church is further enhanced by the unity that is accomplished in Christ among all the members of the Church. This unity is a result of true communion in God and is referred to by the Holy Father as 'solidarity'. Solidarity experienced in this manner by the members of the Church causes greater effectiveness in the communication of the faith."[51]

The Church is called to learn professionalism, excellence, and best practices from Communications Science. Most Catholic communicators, however, will be priests and laypersons who are not communications professionals. The following communications model is for that non-professional 'Everyman' who participates in the communication of Christ. The Church needs those who can design formal public relations, education, media use and other communications strategies and protocols for the furtherance of Her missions. She also is designed to place individual communicators of Christ in millions of specific *loci* throughout time and space, and to equip each one Sacramentally, supernaturally, to realize His presence in place. We turn next toward a practical understanding of theologically grounded, not-too-academic communications theory for the 'middlework' that is yours to do.

---

[50] Dr. Christine Mugridge and Sr. Marie Gannon, *John Paul II Development of a Theology of Communication*, pg. 62
[51] Dr. Christine Mugridge and Sr. Marie Gannon, *John Paul II Development of a Theology of Communication*, pg. 212

**Practical Catholic Communications**

*Definitions and First Principles*

Communication is the process by which Word (or a message with meaning) is transmitted from person to person in some form, such as words, gesture, symbol, or object. Communicants are parties to the process of communication: giving, receiving, and sharing the Gift being communicated. Communication's highest message is Christ's invitation to communion with the Trinity. Communication's most perfect context is loving communion in which Christ Himself is present within the form of community, or human relationship. Communication is communion to the extent Christ – in actuality: Body, Blood, Soul and Divinity (in the Eucharist), Person (in each believer), and Triune Presence (among His people, or in His Church) – is shared (which implies giving *and* receiving Gift, or 'reciprocity') among the communicants.

By the practice of communication, communicators grow in capacity to receive and to transmit Word, or meanings within form. By the practice of community (sharing together in the communication of Christ – that is, receiving Him together in Mass, offering Him to one another reciprocally, and collaborating to communicate Him to others together), communicants grow in capacity to be vessels, together, for the Presence of Christ. The 'meaning' of the message of His Presence is He, Himself.

*Components of Communication*

In this Catholic model, we see three components: Persons, Form (word, act, content), and Context. Rather than a 'transportation' or 'machine' model which focuses on the form (the message is encoded, then decoded; the message is the 'point' of a transaction between a sender and receiver), and in addition to the more complete interpersonal model (which includes the persons emotionally and psychologically as 'contexts' of receptivity, and the whole communication 'environment' as context), the Catholic model necessarily includes a critical difference: God *is*, and intends to be communicated. His instruments are transformed in the process. To some degree, then, we can say that all other kinds of communication have this potential to be transformative for the participants. This potential is another level of meaning within any form of communication, raising the ideal form off the plane of mere exchange of information toward greater dimensionality and integrity of form.

*The Greater Context*

The overarching Catholic 'context' for any communication is the reality of the Trinity: God gave utterance to Christ, a form which utterly conveyed the All-that-God-is and which perfectly is the fulfillment of that All. Proceeding from the perfect correspondence between the Father and the Son, His 'final Word,' the Holy Spirit of Love echoed the infinite Truth of infinity affirmed and fulfilled. There are no words that can encompass such a reality, but we can approach: all-potentiality condescended with all-perfection to become all-actuality; Perfect Love took Perfect Form to be Perfectly Fulfilled; all-Gift was transmitted with all-freedom and all-freely-reciprocated by all-affirmation-and-gratitude (which is 'worship'). Our communication model must be orders of magnitude 'smaller' or 'lower' than the Trinity, but takes its features from this ideal.

Only from within this highest context does our communication model establish 'person' as the place, or *locus* of resolution of tension between content and context. Our 'person' is not just another complicating force in an already complex context. Nor is 'person' simply the object that tosses or catches the all-important 'message'. Person is the context within which meaning blooms from within form, and the one 'object' in Creation capable of placing meaning into forms for the self-donation which fulfills persons. Communication has the potential to be the action-context within which persons experience Christ's response, the relation-context within which they experience His presence, and the form by which both Self and Christ emerge into the world of lived experience and concrete reality.

Each person is both receiver and transmitter, with a unique makeup, structure, or capacity for Word, or for encoding and decoding messages given in forms. Even when there is one speaker and one listener, both communicants are both sending and receiving messages which all affect the 'success' of the communication relationship as to content. Each is also a context, in himself, and a part of the overall 'communication environment'. We may reduce communications to the formation and exchange of 'content,' 'information,' or 'message' for simplification, but will need a more complete frame of reference to do justice to the persons involved.

*Too Complex, Too Simple*

We persons are a) forms God designed by means of which to communicate Himself, b) contexts within which 'message' becomes 'meaning,' and c) actors, relators, communicants who may come into union with other persons in a way that invites 'message' to take 'form' in our midst. The forms we create to exchange meaning are a) simple verbal and material structures that convey simple messages, information, or meaning (such as a STOP sign, an invitation to a party, or a thumbs-up emoticon), b) gifts by means of which we, ourselves, are given as a higher order 'message' transmitted alongside whatever simple information is, literally, given (such as a plate of cookies that says "I love you," or a two-hour face-to-face conversation that gives *presence* in addition to whatever topic was discussed), and c) signs by means of which we offer entrance into the shared experience of reality (such as a ritual of re-enactment, and such as a poem or painting that wraps my experience of pain or of a sunrise in words or color-and-shape and conveys to you, in my voice or style, some taste of the way I was moved or touched). The context of communication is a) spatial, physical, material, b) historical, or temporal and c) spiritual, thus eternal.

Each of the three components of communication has the potential to be fulfilled in the process, or raised to its own highest degree of correspondence to Christ. Persons, raised to the highest degree of Christ-likeness, are characterized by holiness, virtue, and freedom. Any movement toward these qualities accomplished through communication is, thus, an indicator of an improvement in the process. We call it simply a movement toward Goodness. Word (any act, or form by which we convey meaning) reaches its highest fulfillment in the Person of Christ, who is Truth. An evaluation of content as a component of communication considers both its intrinsic degree of Truth and also the degree to which it is transmitted/received without degradation or corruption. The context of communication has the potential to be 'full of grace,' 'loving,' 'symphonic,' and 'seamless' – all phrases that suggest its correspondence to the transcendent quality of Beauty.

Even the simplicity of 'three components' grows quite complex, on closer inspection.

In the process of communication, the persons involved give the gift of Self, to some degree, along with the content, or message being transmitted. The self-giving of persons accumulates between them over time as context, community, culture. Thus, what seems to be an empty space between them (or a silence until a message enters it) is actually quite full of an invisible matrix that supports, shapes, influences, and interferes with the process of communication. The accumulation of old messages gradually becomes a part of the context within which new messages are conveyed. Thus content becomes context and context becomes content in a constant flux that sometimes acts as background noise to silence a message, but now and then serves to amplify a message in a way that defies analysis.

*We Reweave the Middle Ground*

Communication participates in, or corresponds to, a sphere far beyond our comprehension. We approach it through intimate, personal conversations, formal and organizational communications, cultural and technology-mediated communications, and sacramental/liturgical participation. We can fly into the upper atmosphere, but must come down the ladder of proportions to the person-centered, place-bound, concrete work of improving all our communications from the very small place and particularity we each inhabit. We can look 'down' at communications patterns, models and systems without losing sight of the higher context. We can look 'up' or 'through' human communications to the divine pattern without ignoring the need to develop and evaluate actual skills and actual forms for more effective communications.

We dwell in the 'middle' for the most part, and our communications help to strengthen that middle: the civil sphere where respectful disagreement may occur in the pursuit of truth, the social fabric of local and national life, the gaps between polarized positions and people alienated from one another. Middlework is the work of moving, communicating back and forth across those deserts and voids, by means of words and relationships, weaving people together with the doctrines and ideas that lead to integral human development and the common good.

Whatever we do to improve our communications – our skills, our messages, ourselves as effective contexts, etc ... – improves our ability to communicate Christ. Because it is the mission of the Church – a community of persons – to extend outward to communicate on a global level, or with those 'afar off,' we must improve ourselves as communities in order to collaborate in that mission. Not everyone will be called, or have opportunity to exercise apologetic skill or public speaking ability, or to interact with a very-different culture. But however far you are asked to extend, you help build the Church's 'extension strength' when you build the 'core strength' of life in Christian community at the local, personal level.

## Unity and Responsibility

*You are Responsible*

The individual person is a center – an attractive *gravitas* of actuality, a node or hub in a vast network of communications, a radiant beacon whose acts of freedom

become invitations to Christ, a healthy cell in a Body.
You – that individual, that form – are the tiny, powerless
'transmitting tower' resounding Christ into the world.
Why does it matter how well, how truly, how beautifully,
how lovingly, how effectively you communicate?
Because you reside within an amplifying structure – the
Church – it matters very much. As Christ dwells in you,
resounding, you dwell in the Church, within which His
voice, particularized in your own, resounds. Your qualities,
your acts, your creations, your communications matter,
not because of your greatness and enormity, but because
Christ has chosen to use your humility and nothingness as
the means that, collected into unity within His Body, will
greatly affect the world.

In a way (a small way…don't worry!), you are responsible
for the rescue of those perishing around you.

The quality of our middlework involves the degree to
which love flows through our hearts to those with whom
we communicate. Learning to be 'we' within family and
Church gives us practice with Others who are most like us
in language, shared experience, beliefs and values. As a
member of the Body, we speak for ourselves and for Christ
– voicing, through our own free acts, His response to the
realities we face. The Church then, through her members,
acts as an interface between Christ and the world – between
'we' and 'them'. You need not feel burdened by all the
need in the world, but only realize that you are capable
of responding to whatever you actually face. You are
response-able, because you are free.

In the individual, the capacity to resonate with Truth
and to correspond to Reality is 'freedom'. In the Body,

the capacity to resound the Word and bring it into correspondence with the human beings we encounter is 'unity'. *Freedom* is to the individual as *unity* is to the community: a capacity to receive and give love in act, gesture, words, and other forms. The middlework of building strong community makes of our 'we' a vessel for the communication of Christ.

*We are Responsible*

The Body is the means, the Church is the context of the message that is Christ, Himself. He is communicated first to His people, and then through them – by His own design – to those who do not know Him. She is the essential support structure, or matrix, for our formation in freedom and unity.

Through the Church, through Mary, the Holy Spirit is working in the world to draw all men to the Father through the Son. The Body of the Son, His Church, His people, is given to the world to call all men into unity with the Lord of Love. "…the presence of the Christian Fact lies in the unity of believers. …Thus we see the method, characteristic of that Fact, for "converting" the world: that this unity be made visible, everywhere. In the absence of this unity, no Christian religiosity can stand. …That sense of community, of charity, of unity, that is, that sense of the one, catholic – or universal – Church must grow in us. …Christ is realized in us and among us through our companionship.[52]

There is a work within the Church called, officially, "The Work of Mary". Less formally known as 'Focolare,' the Movement's particular charism, its emphasis for our times,

---

[52] Luigi Giussani, *Religious Awareness in Modern Man*, pg. 33, 34

is the promotion of the deep unity among persons for which Christ suffered Himself to be utterly forsaken on the Cross. The amazing success of this work is just one example of the operation of the Holy Spirit through Mary, through the Church, through God's people. There are now Anglicans, Jews, Buddhists, and Muslims learning from Catholic Focolare the way of love, and the unity that is possible when we lay down our lives for one another.

Chiara Lubich, Focolare's foundress, taught that the willingness to participate in Christ's own forsakenness on the Cross is the key to unity. What must we forsake to bring unity with our neighbor? Pride? Power? Indifference? Fear? Self-righteousness? Lubich says:

> It is a matter of momentarily putting aside even the most beautiful and greatest things we have: our own faith, our own convictions, in order to be 'nothing' in front of the other person, a 'nothingness of love'. By doing so we put ourselves in an attitude of learning, and in reality we always do have something to learn. ...We enter their world, in some way we become inculturated in them and we are enriched. ...Our complete openness and acceptance then predisposes the other person to listen to us. We have noticed, in fact, that when people see someone dying to self in order to 'make him or herself one' with others, they are struck by this and often ask for an explanation. This leads us then to what the Pope calls 'respectful proclamation.' 'Respect' is the key word in every dialogue. Being true to God, to ourselves, and being sincere with our neighbor, we share what our faith affirms on the subject

we are discussing, without imposing anything, without any trace of proselytism, but only out of love. ...Real, true, heart-felt fraternity is, in fact, the fruit of a love capable of making itself dialogue, relationship, that is, a love that, far from arrogantly closing itself within its own boundaries, opens itself toward others and works together with all people of goodwill in order to build together unity and peace in the world.[53]

*Love is Essential*

Love, without which our best theology is empty of meaning, must be the basis of our attempts to build and live in unity with others. To be one with the loving heart of God, we can do no better than follow Mary's example. When Jesus wanted to draw all men to Himself, and gave up His life on the Cross, He left His own Mother to be the Mother of All the Living – a new Eve to restore the brooding, hovering, creating, comforting, communicating love of the Holy Spirit to all the world's children. Whenever Mary is seen, or heard, or portrayed, she is pointing to the moment of Christ's self-abandonment as the key to unity with Him. Like a true mother, she would gather us all under her wing and present us to Him as *one*. The enemy sows fear and division. The mother sows love, and teaches us to be united to others in love.

Within the family, the friendship, the community, the Church, we learn to be *one*. Christ yearned for us to be *one*

---

[53] Lubich, Chiara. "360 Dialogue." In *Essential Writings: Spirituality, Dialogue, Culture*, translated by Michel Vandeleene, 320-359. Hyde Park, N.Y.: New City Press, 2007, pg. 340.

even as He and the Father and the Holy Spirit are *one*.[54] We are invited to the Great Love within the Trinity, and these small practice grounds give us a taste of the goodness of that Love who beckons us forward. These are hard places, full of imperfect people who are hard to love and who have difficulty loving us. Here, we are vulnerable (literally: *wound*-able) and so here, we practice forgiveness most frequently. The image of a place of belonging that does not involve this real hardship and practice of forgiveness is an illusion being sold through sit-coms and movies and social media's public-facing personas. To turn away from life in the family, or from life in community within the Church, is to turn away from the cultivation of love.

To open your heart to that Other is to give him place within yourself. As you emulate the Blessed Mother's heart-hospitality, you fight for the rescue of souls from the atomization and isolation in which they are drowning. "The evil of our times consists in the first place in a kind of degradation, indeed in a pulverization, of the fundamental uniqueness of each human person. This evil is even much more of the metaphysical than of the moral order. To this disintegration, planned at times by atheistic ideologies, we must oppose, rather than sterile polemics, a kind of "recapitulation" of the mystery of the person."[55] Mary's gaze is always the gaze of love. She is a place of encounter with the One who is Peace. In her, we see our own mission to be a place of encounter for our neighbors with Christ. If you have trouble seeing others through the eyes of love, ask for her longing for their souls to be communicated into your own soul.

---

[54] See the Gospel of St. John, Chapter 17, where Jesus prays that we may be one, even as He and the Father are one.
[55] St. Pope John Paul II, in a letter to Henri de Lubac, 1968

*Unity is the Atmosphere of Love*

The manifest unity of Christians is the Church – the very Body of the Lord God. In order to extend the one-ness of God into the world, we must be in unity with His Church. *One* is the beginning of common ground between us. In Him, we all live and move and have our being. He makes it possible for us to live in unity with each other. Christians are called to make manifest His one-ness by extending this unity, this kingdom of reconciling love, this message that peace is possible to our neighbors – for love of Him who has first loved us.

Our words, acts, institutions and works of art place us 'in dialogue with' others. Our arguments for Catholic Faith and moral choices, and our reasons for hope are meant to be communicated. Christ is meant to be shared through our engagement with others. At the root of our ability to engage in dialogue as a spiritual practice is the authenticity of our own encounter with Christ, our own humility and awareness of Christ's presence as essential to life. Unity should characterize our relations with the Body of Christ and with our fellow man. There is simply no basis for that supernatural, cohesive quality but the very utmost self-donation of Christ to us, expressed most completely in the moment, on the Cross, when He experienced the very sense of abandonment by God that is at the origin of all human suffering.

When we, through the love and grace afforded to us by this unimaginable gift of God, hold ourselves in unity with others, we express our identification with Christ on the Cross, and thus lift up His Cross again and again as a beacon of light in a darkened world. It is He who draws all men to himself through His Real Presence in the midst of those who love Him. Our unity with others creates a vessel for that Presence in the world. Christ, and our Church, commissions us to involve ourselves in dialogue that challenges and strengthens our own faith as it plants and cultivates seeds of faith in others. The duty and privilege Love has placed upon us is to take the risk of loving – building bridges, investing in relationship and community, becoming peacemakers and servants.

*Community is the Context that Opens Outward*

Life within a people animated by Christ's presence in and among them is made possible when they offer the gift of their unity as a 'place' for persons 'displaced' from unity, integrity, truth, and freedom. This life in community as the Body of Christ is essential for the cultivation of persons who possess interior unity, integrity and freedom. "The promotion of unity belongs to the innermost nature of the Church, for she is …a sacramental sign and an instrument of intimate union with God, and of the unity of the whole human race."[56]

If we first seek unity within the Church, we may better offer Christ fully to the world. The life of the Body of Christ is measured by the strength of its unity, "just as dissociation and dispersion are the measure of death."[57]

The Church is, in fact, a community, but should also become, in actual practice, a communion of persons. Lay communities, families, universities, parish churches, and other groups all enhance the Church's awareness of itself as community, and can foster the growth of their members

---

[56] *Gaudium et spes*, 42
[57] Luigi Giussani, *The Journey to Truth is an Experience*, pg. 31

in communion. Christ, loved in His Body, in the midst of His people, is Christ realized more fully than He can be realized in a merely "individual" relationship. Through the Work of Mary, a deeper understanding of what it takes to live in communion has developed for the benefit of the whole Church. Having learned to live the spirituality of unity in small Focolare communities, Focolare members were prepared to respond to the Holy Father's plea for unity among various lay movements in the Church. Chiara Lubich said that the focus changed for her companions – from each individual getting to God, to each one concerned with all the community getting to God.

The whole, free, integrated Catholic is the one in full unity with the Church, sharing Christ's desire for unity in His Body. This person becomes an expression of Christ in the world more fully than if he spoke merely for his own private relationship with Christ. In the Church, there is room for other persons. Into a personal relationship with Christ (important as that is to the individual), others are not invited. Theology detached from full incorporation into the life of believers is barren. We can only teach what we live. If we live in the freedom and the unity of Christ, we will realize community. Once community is a lived reality among us, we can share the principle of unity with others. Culture is the priority of the New Evangelization because it proclaims Truth in a lived, embodied way that provides a medium for dialogue, or place of exchange between 'us' and 'them'. We'll look at communication with culture, or for cultural renewal, in Chapter 10.

Chapter 5

# We-They: Love is the Context of Dialogue

Dialogue – the practice and spirit of genuine interest in others – is the means of renewing the culture. It represents a refusal to harden our hearts to others, to allow them to be demonized, to accept a marginal and passive role for the Church, or to despair for the salvation of the souls we encounter. Francis Cardinal George tells us, "To enter dialogue is to embrace the humility of the Crucified Jesus while demonstrating the wonder of crucified love."[58]

The Truth that will set men free cannot remain abstract. True words need something like a 'container,' or context, in order to be shared. German Catholic philosopher Josef Pieper indicates that dialogue is the vessel for truth: "The natural habitat of truth is found in interpersonal communication. Truth lives in dialogue, in discussion, in conversation. It resides, therefore, in language, in the word."[59] Fr. Luigi Giussani tells us "communication that has become appealing and evocative is the beginning of the cultural phenomenon; it is the fire that ignites it."[60] We need to communicate – generate forms and give them – in ways that light fire in the midst of persons. We need to be radically affected by Christ ourselves so that His Presence draws others into encounter with Him through our interaction.

---

[58] Cardinal Francis George, *The Difference God Makes*, pg. 106
[59] Josef Pieper, *The Abuse of Language*, pg. 36
[60] Luigi Giussani, *The Journey to Truth is an Experience*, pg. 31

Excellence in dialogue is the fruit of spiritual maturity, passion, preparation, verbal and relational skills, and constant recourse to the help of the Holy Spirit. All of this develops through intentionality, life experience, practice and hard work. No amount of work, or of doctrinal knowledge, or rhetorical ability can substitute for the spirit of dialogue – the interior quality of readiness to encounter a person and to engage him. The qualities of personal freedom and interpersonal unity 'drape' all our content in the flow of Love, which is the ultimate context.

St. Pope John Paul II called dialogue "the art of spiritual communication." It does not have to be 'religious talk,' or 'faith topics' to be 'spiritual'. What makes it 'spiritual communication' is the love cloaking all we say in an atmosphere of unity, respect, peace, and dignity. "Dialogue does not extend exclusively to matters of doctrine, but engages the whole person; it is also a dialogue of love." [61] What makes dialogue an 'art' is that in our communication, we create a resolution of the tension between Self and Other, between 'us' and 'them,' between listening and speaking, between the ideal of Christ (or abstract knowledge of Him) and the actuality of His presence, by virtue of our own presence to a person.

If you are genuinely interested in the other person, you should realize you will be affected by them – dismayed by finding great differences, and also attracted to the truth, beauty and goodness you find in those whose beliefs you cannot share. Good preparation should help you to expect a 'beautiful adventure' as you enter into dialogue, give you ideas about fruitful areas of discussion to open on the basis of the other person's beliefs, help you navigate delicate

---

[61] *Ut Unum Sint*, 28

areas of difference without causing or taking offense, and prevent you becoming confused and disoriented about your own beliefs while learning of theirs. "By preparing ourselves for dialogue, even if none takes place, we deepen our contemplation of the truth that it has been granted us to know. And if the dialogue is genuine (not merely a disguised attempt to convert), it will be a search for those truths we ourselves do not yet possess or fully understand, and which turn up in the most unexpected places. Dialogue…does not require us first to agree on the doctrine of the Trinity."[62]

**Dia-logic Makes a *Via Media***

The tension between Self and Other grows as the distance to the Other from our own self-identity increases. Simply to pay attention (to be tensed toward the Other in love) begins to turn the unity we offer into a mediating structure, or path. "Attention is the rarest and purest form of generosity," said Simone Weil. The tension is not a 'negative,' (though it may make us feel uncomfortable) but is a creative potential from which emerges the path unique to the persons in this present dialogue.

The gulf between us grows wider the harder it is to find common ground. If we begin from polarized positions and a prejudicial or self-defensive wariness, we may see dialogue as weak compromise and have greater difficulty finding a path to the Other (as a *person*, not a *position*). Love makes a way where there is no way[63]. Christ himself is the Way to unity with the

---

[62] Stratford Caldecott, *The Radiance of Being*, pg. 191
[63] "…I am making a way in the desert and streams in the wasteland." Isaiah 43:19

Other, allowing us to approach him as a deep mystery, deserving of dignity, with no fear for ourselves that sets up a barrier between us. Our fearlessness is not to be a proud self-reliance, or a reckless self-endangerment, but a reasonable trust in Christ who loves us both and desires to draw us closer to Himself through this encounter.

Hans Urs von Balthasar, in *Convergences*, suggests that dialogue emerges from our theological contemplation, moving outward in our attempts to proclaim what we believe, and finally meets the person who is 'outside' the boundary of our self-definition or identity – leading back step-by-step from 'outside' to 'inside' in loving companionship. We are able to shift the center of 'self' outward to identify with and accompany him. "Love is creative for the fellow man; it produces an image of him with which the beloved would not have credited himself, and when love is genuine and faithful, it gives him the power to come closer to this image or make himself like it. …A Christian never has his unity within himself; nor does he in any way seek it in himself. He does not collect himself around his own center, but rather wholly elsewhere. 'The life I live now is not my own; Christ is living in me.'…(Gal 2:20)…my failing, guilty I, …in his Cross and death…in that event, it is settled and put behind me, and my real, actual believed-in-and-hoped-for-I lives *in him* and comes to me from him."[64]

The particular religious, ethnic, national, generational, political, historical, familial, educational, social and technological contexts forming any individual make it impossible to learn a pre-fabricated template for dialogue with everyone. The reality of the mysterious and wonderful

---

[64] Hans Urs von Balthasar, *Convergences*, pg.129

multiplicity of persons who surround us frustrates any attempt to unilaterally prepare a response to them in advance. We need to *learn* our faith, to *become ready and able* to "give an answer,"[65] and to *practice* civility in disagreement, formal apologetics, cordial conversation, and robust argumentation. But to be a presence that leads to Christ, we must be present as one deep mystery to another, without the self-defenses of preconceptions, prepared speeches, fill-in-the-blank answers, and knee-jerk reactions.

"In this dialogue he must humanly and personally make himself vulnerable…Dialogical theology, as opposed to kerygmatic, is no longer a theology which thinks from inside to outside, but rather one which leads step by step, in conversation with the brother, from outside to inside: a theology in the form of a *theologia crucis*, not merely by virtue of an inner (formal-logical) paradox, but of an existential realization, especially in the Christian, who can open to the Lord the other person's final otherness in being and thinking, no longer through words and arguments, but through…a silent, accompanying witness."[66]

## Use Dialogic Techniques with Caution

We need to become people who can *respond* as encounter, as a question, as dialogue occurs. Dialogue can never be reduced to techniques, though some techniques may be instructive and help our dialogue to be more effective as a means of persuasion.

---

[65] 1 Peter 3:15: "But sanctify the Lord God in your hearts: and be ready always to give an answer to every man that asketh you a reason of the hope that is in you with meekness and fear."
[66] See Hans Urs von Balthasar, *Convergences*, Chapter 2

A quick online search will turn up many, many references to dialogue from within various areas of culture. Much work has been done in the corporate and philanthropic spheres to develop dialogic approaches to problem solving and idea generation. Educators and coaches have developed many dialogic variations on the ancient Socratic dialogue. Civic dialogue, public discourse, or civic engagement is being promoted through an array of methods, or processes, such as Town Meeting, Charrettes, Citizen Choicework, Deliberative Polling, and Conversation Café.[67]

Among these many methods are to be found techniques that might be helpful to you in designing formal conversation opportunities with groups of various sizes, interests and purposes. Some seem more skewed than others toward pressing – in the name of mutual respect, or diversity – a social agenda that, at best, is "shallow ecumenism," and, at worst, is hostile to a Catholic understanding of excellent interreligious dialogue. The goal that may drive more public conversations (a problem solution is needed, an agreement to act collaboratively must be reached, a decision must be made), should not characterize personal dialogue among individuals building ongoing relationships.

A goal orientation can, if it becomes an interior demand, reduce your freedom and thus, your capacity to offer unity, or self-as-safe-place as a context for dialogue. One of the contemporary models for dialogue (and one that deeply influences many others) is Appreciative Inquiry (AI).

I offer a small,cautionary critique of AI due to its wide use and potential for misuse. In general, AI participants are

---

[67] The National Coalition for Dialogue and Deliberation offers comparison of and training in all these and more.

encouraged to move away from talk of problems, solutions and analysis toward talk of strengths, opportunities, and positive examples. AI is based upon several core principles, which practitioners implement as facilitators for different kinds of team-building, issue-resolution, or visioning conversations in families, corporations, and communities. The core principles, in brief, are:

- The Constructionist Principle – Reality, as we know it, is a subjective state socially created through language and conversations.

- The Simultaneity Principle – Inquiry Creates Change. The moment we ask a question, we begin to create a change.

- The Poetic Principle – What we choose to study makes a difference. It describes – even creates – the world as we know it.

- The Anticipatory Principle – Human systems move in the direction of their images of the future. The more positive and hopeful the image of the future, the more positive the present-day action.

- The Positive Principle – Momentum for change requires large amounts of positive affect and social bonding. This momentum is best generated through positive questions that amplify the positive core.[68]

In some applications of AI, the idea of constructivism seems close to 'positive thinking,' or 'using imagination to address issues creatively.' In this sense, there is no

---

[68] CenterforAppreciativeInquiry.net

conflict with Catholic thought. However, in some contexts, the principle undermines Catholic teachings about social realities and, indeed, undermines reality itself. It is one thing to "allow others in the conversation to have their beliefs without resistance" as AI practitioner Jacqueline Bascobert Kelm suggests.[69] It is another to believe, with Kelm, that my strong personal beliefs about God are "my local truth," and have no foundation in objective reality.[70] We must listen and learn from others how they "view a situation and the meaning they develop."[71] We must "reflect on our taken-for-granted thoughts".[72] And we must look for the good, the right, and the beautiful in a person or situation.[73] But we must not accept that our "traditional belief that reality is something we observe rather than create" is now outdated.[74]

We can and should recognize that our mental models and filters, observational weaknesses, emotional projections, interpretations of others' symbols, confirmation biases, conscious choices about framing and focus, and other aspects of perception give us enormous scope for volitional control over the openness we bring to a conversation, dialogue, or discussion. This awareness is critical to getting the Self out of the way of loving openness to the Other, but should not extend to the elimination of the boundary of Self entirely.

---

[69] Jacqueline Bascobert Kelm, *Appreciative Living*, pg. 21
[70] Jacqueline Bascobert Kelm, *Appreciative Living*, pg. 18
[71] Jacqueline Bascobert Kelm, *Appreciative Living*, pg. 21
[72] Jacqueline Bascobert Kelm, *Appreciative Living*, pg. 21
[73] Jacqueline Bascobert Kelm, *Appreciative Living*, pg. 31 and Philippians 4:8
[74] Jacqueline Bascobert Kelm, *Appreciative Living*, pg. 32)

You only are a *presence* because you are an actual, real, separate, unique, unrepeatable, knowable *person*, and are only able to accompany the Other toward Christ because He is a Person who actually exists and is, in himself, an instance of objective reality. Your Self is not only 'in the way,' but is actually the veiled presence of a light that shines through your mediation. One might as well say "Get the filament out of the way of the light in that bulb" as say "Get your Self to be a non-reality so the Other will feel unthreatened."

I actually have great appreciation for the lessons AI teaches about bringing positivity and vulnerability to the exchange between persons. My caution is that it sometimes becomes an insistence that nothing 'negative' ever be said, and can overlook the role of a person (imperfect, of course) in being exactly the 'structure' that best mediates Christ to an Other. I agree that it is less helpful to frame a situation as 'problem solving' than to face it squarely, with optimism and courage, and respond creatively. The best respondent, however, is the free human person, who has learned to "correspond to reality in the totality of its factors."[75] and thus is open to the Divine Person who communicates Himself (the reality of whom is not dependent on how strongly I believe in Him).

Note that freedom involves the integration of objective and subjective reality – not merely the subjectivization of all reality. The reality you see, however frankly you face it, however thoroughly you analyze and describe it, however consciously you accept it, is incomplete. You can humbly acknowledge that your mind cannot *comprehend* all reality,

---

[75] Fr. Luigi Giussani: "Freedom is the correspondence to reality, in the totality of its factors."

while believing that you *correspond* to all reality through the One who holds it all in being. It is not a subjective belief, but an objective truth that Christ is the Word at the origin of all reality, and the final Word of its complete fulfillment. Hope, that most positive atmosphere, opens to the totality of reality's factors, through Christ.

More study would be needed for an effective critique, but this is just an example of moving into dialogic techniques carefully. Similarly, involvement with other dialogic techniques could be very helpful if a preliminary critical evaluation could first be done. Over-emphasis on technique can overburden the form ('dialogue,' 'conversation,' etc...), or flatten it into a two-dimensional exchange that limits its capacity to promote personhood and freedom.

Turning, again, toward the human person (as a Catholic wisdom must do), we see how communication may take us far beyond exchange by lifting us through tensions (instead of eliminating tensions) to resolution on a higher plane.

**Wisdom Moves Toward Love**

Our work in words takes us from intimate conversation among family and friends to wider circles which are less and less *of* the persons within, as they grow more and more *about* whatever interest, profession, or other focus those persons share. The more homogenous the persons, the more we feel belonging, We-ness, and safety in conversation with them. Conversely, the more heterogeneity, the more They-ness, the less of this subjective quality of ease we may feel. Tensions rise with the degree of Other-ness and as the context seems to disintegrate, the persons making it up follow their own self-defense strategies.

We may over-focus on content as a distraction from the discomfort of the context. We can implode into a context with no space for much content (for example, the friendship in which some topics are never discussed), or fracture into identification with content instead of each other (the friendship that becomes a means to get a project done, for instance). Pressure to conform to the group, or to prove mastery of the content may result. As a substitute for authentic, organic belonging, we create inner rings with our specialized knowledge and jargon. The less real We-ness we feel, the more belonging, or fitting into The Group matters. Its definition, rules, norms, and membership requirements (whether explicit, or implicit) provide the interiority of boundary (or We-ness), and some sense of safety.

Unless love is the ultimate 'meaning' and value of being together, people in such groups as clubs, churches, and other civic associations or identity categories tend to handle their tensions with either more and more rigid rules, or with movement toward fracturing into smaller subsets. The more freedom in each person present to a conversation, the less the group will develop these fearful contraction characteristics. Love, of course, is the answer to the fear that motivates all that self-defensiveness. "Perfect love casts out fear." (1 John 4:18)

Dialogue is the art of spiritual communication because such communication invites the Spirit into the vessel of your unity with these Others, to play a 'new note' upon the tensions offered up to Him. *Dia + Logos*: The Word, piercing, communicating, coming, through one human being to another. Love's presence registers with participants as warmth, affection, mutual interest, trust, personal safety, ease, and graciousness. The more 'open channels' – free human persons – through whom Love is communicated, the richer the context becomes. Such richness is what is meant by the term 'communio'.

The universal communion of all men is a gift given by God. Our life in community as the Church, and in various communities of interest, vocation, or locality, is predicated upon the Catholic belief that God has established this communion through Christ. Our ability to engage in common activity, conversation, and even to struggle through conflict to real communication and resolution, depends on the reality that this communion with others is possible. These ideas, expressed in "Communio – A Program," by Hans Urs von Balthasar, opened the door on a contemporary cultural project (The Communio International Catholic Review journal, established in 1972) that has been tremendously influential in helping to reunite Catholic tradition and the post-conciliar Church through dialogue.[76]

As with conversation, dialogue is a skill we can both learn about and improve upon. As we participate, our personhood takes on dimension that, to a growing degree, allows for the presence of persons. Persons we encounter can, increasingly, be allowed entrance, welcomed in, to the context that is 'me,' or 'us'. Fr. Giussani highlights this transformation of the instrument through the process of communication:

> Our dialogue is the mutual communication of ourselves through the signs of words, gesture, and attitudes: the emphasis is not on ideas, but on the person as such, on freedom. Our dialogue is life, and ideas are one expression of this life. …Dialogue

---

[76] See Hans Urs von Balthasar, "Communio: A Program" in Communio International Catholic Review, Vol. 33.1

is communicating one's own personal life to other personal lives; dialogue is sharing the existence of others in one's own existence; it is a gift of self. In a dialogue you give what you have. So the more you give, the more you have a personality, the more mature you are. The first sign of maturity is awareness and consciousness of your own being. The more you are aware of your own human experience, the more mature you are.[77]

**Rules are Tension-Bearing Structures**

Just as the rules of courtesy are means by which love may be carried into practice, into actuality, or into form, other formal rules for conversations and dialogue of various kinds help provide for the successful resolution of the tensions they inevitably bring about. As G.K. Chesterton observed, the limiting fence makes the playground possible, and the frame is of the essence of a work of art.[78] As we make of our lives and conversations works of co-operative art, they rise to receive and embody higher meaning, transformative resolution, and love.

---

[77] Luigi Giussani, *The Journey to Truth is an Experience*, pg. 35

[78] G.K. Chesterton: "Catholic doctrine and discipline may be walls; but they are the walls of a playground. Christianity is the only frame which has preserved the pleasure of Paganism. We might fancy some children playing on the flat grassy top of some tall island in the sea. So long as there was a wall round the cliff's edge they could fling themselves into every frantic game and make the place the noisiest of nurseries. But the walls were knocked down, leaving the naked peril of the precipice. They did not fall over; but when their friends returned to them they were all huddled in terror in the centre of the island; and their song had ceased."; "Art is limitation; the essence of every picture is the frame." (In *Orthodoxy*)

It's helpful to articulate not only the rules for belonging and engagement, but also to remind participants of the ground rules for courtesy and civility. Margaret Shepherd, in *The Art of Civilized Conversation*, suggests these as starters:

> ...civilized conversation is not the same as reciting, confessing, negotiating, scolding, or interviewing. It does not involve notifying, debating, or issuing orders, nor does it include baiting, shouting, hurling personal insults, contradicting, grandstanding, or interrupting. It does not require a referee. It is most surely not what people hear on many television and radio talk shows: that is performance art of particular emptiness, and the worst example of how to converse.[79]

Mortimer Adler, in *Some Rules for Good Conversation*, offers a helpful rule for handling disagreement:

> The first rule to be followed is this. Do not disagree – or, for that matter, do not agree – with anyone else unless you are sure you understand the position the other person is taking. To disagree before you understand is impertinent. To agree is inane. To make sure that you understand, before you disagree, exercise the courtesy of asking the other person the following question: "Do I understand you to say that…?...you must continue with the question and answer procedure until the other tells you that you have at last caught the point, that you understand him precisely as he wishes to be understood. Only then do you have the grounds indispensable for intelligent and reasonable

---

[79] *The Art of Civilized Conversation*, Margaret Shepherd, Sharon Hogan, Broadway Books, NJ, 2005, pg. 3

> disagreement or agreement. This procedure is time consuming. It requires patience and persistence. Most people anxious to get on with the discussion bypass it. ...They are satisfied with merely apparent disagreements or agreements, instead of seeking a genuine meeting of minds.[80]

That excellent communication requires patience is a point worth repeating. David Baily Harned, in *Patience*, has this to say:

> The issue is very simple. If life is dialogue, mutuality, and responsiveness, then patience is at its center. ...there has been consistent agreement within the Christian tradition that impatience does not signify merely the absence of a single virtue but the erosion of them all. ...it renders the self vulnerable to the whole spectrum of vices. ...What must we acquire if we are to find a rewarding and enjoyable life? Patience is much of the answer.[81]

Among Stephen Carter's fifteen rules for reconstructing civility are these gems:

- Our duty to be civil toward others does not depend on whether we like them or not.

- Civility has two parts: generosity, even when it is costly, and trust, even when there is risk.

- We must come into the presence of our fellow human beings with a sense of awe and gratitude.

---

[80] *Some Rules for Good Conversation*, Mortimer Adler, from the Adler Archive at radicalacademy.com/adlerconversation.htm

[81] David Baily Harned, *Patience*, Chapter 1

- Teaching civility, by word and example, is an obligation of the family. The state must not interfere with the family's effort to create a coherent moral universe for its children.[82]

New rules result in new forms, such as Book Groups, Therapy Circles, Jefferson Dinners, debates, panel discussion, pecha kucha presentations, memes, TED talks, etc… that help bridge between We's and They's, taking us further into the public, or cultural domain. In Chapter 11 – The Possibilities of Form, we'll discuss these new forms of context and of content. Before we move toward the external structure of various forms of conversation, let's take a deeper dive into the formation of structure within the We-They dynamic, where contexts become content, and vice-versa.

**We-They**

Like any form, conversations (discussions, dialogues) have both an 'exterior' structure and an 'interior' dynamic. The presence of persons makes unique demands upon us that reveal our own structural flaws, or disintegration of Self. To the degree we sense safety in the social environment, we relax Self-boundary, express Self more freely, and expand in receptivity to the Others involved. Conversely, to the degree we feel any danger, we tighten up and guard boundary, are wary of free expression, and contract in capacity to let Others 'in,' where they might wound us, or encounter Christ.

---

[82] *Civility*, Stephen L. Carter, Basic Books, NY, 1998, pg. 279

## We-They Begins in the Body

The vagus nerve – a long, crucial nerve which runs vertically parallel to the spine - affects all major organs and controls the autonomic nervous system (ANS). The ANS, operating pre- or sub-cognitively, activates the sympathetic nervous system (SNS), or the parasympathetic nervous system (PNS) in response to danger/safety signals received by the vagus nerve in a non-verbal, non-logical kind of 'knowing by resonance'. The primary sense of safety is triggered by the body language of social engagement – an intricate back-and-forth 'dance' of eye contact, support responses (See Chapter 3 – Conversation), and mimesis (mutual copying of facial expressions, body movements, and sounds). We-ness is processed by the body, and not by the verbal/logical mind. I may find myself wary of you without having any understanding why, and actually place myself in real danger if my self-talk makes me discount that signal.[83] When you perceive my guardedness, lack of eye contact or interest, or fear, your own vagal wariness of me may easily be triggered.

It's important to understand that the We-They dynamic begins in the body, in a concrete way, where vagal response is a next-step of being-moved-we-know-not-why. The physical and emotional reaction is not a mere social construct, a cognitive understanding of the situation, or a spiritual 'sign' that we should bond with or avoid this person. We can learn to notice our own and others' sense of safety as a part of lovingly adjusting the environment to some degree. Others may or may not be able, when feeling fear, to articulate that reality to themselves, or to us, or even

---

[83] See Gavin de Becker, *The Gift of Fear*

to identify it as fear. We may resent the strange demands now being made in the name of personal safety – no trigger words or behaviors, no male voices, no disagreement, insistence upon formulaic 'creedal' agreements about the nature of reality, etc... – but should understand that the root phenomenon of all this fearfulness is poor vagal tone.

A fully therapeutic discussion of vagal modulation is beyond the scope of this book, but Everyman would do well to have some degree of understanding of the dynamic, some skill at modulating his own vagal tone, and some willingness to read the cues that others need his help modulating theirs. Healthy vagal tone is a fully integrated spectrum of responsiveness to reality. Weak vagal tone is 'disintegrated' to some degree, so that a person may suddenly experience acute fear in the absence of actual present danger, dissociation from Self due to unresolved traumatic response, global panic as a false path to coherence – all with no ability to cognitively, verbally, consciously modulate the state of being back to a centered, integrated, poised, free place of fearlessness and correspondence to reality.

Your own strength to engage in potentially uncomfortable interactions comes primarily through participation in the Sacraments, and nurture of the life of Christ within your own person. Your efforts to cultivate freedom – healthy vagal tone, verbal access to reflect on and adjust your own state of being, interior spaciousness and capacity to receive and respond to others – will help Love to flow through your receptive, communicative, well-formed form, and to "cast out fear" in social interactions of all kinds.[84] Doing your best – even to invite the Holy Spirit to move through you,

---

[84] 1 John 4:18: "There is no fear in love; but perfect love casts out fear, because fear involves torment. But he who fears has not been made perfect in love."

your words, your forms – will not be enough to bridge all distances. That is information to use in failing forward, and should not become a temptation to despair.

The 'burden' of love is on the shoulders of the stronger, the older, the wiser, the more mature, or the one on higher ground. The moment you realize you are, whatever your age, the 'adult,' with respect to a 'child' in conversation, or the 'more reasonable' to the 'less sane,' the one in greater correspondence to reality, or the one whose power, strength, or advantage is somewhat threatening to the Other, you're 'it'! Love condescends to meet the Other[85] to modulate its expression of power, to find a path to understanding, to generate verbal structures that show respect and willingness to be influenced, to lay down even being 'right' for the sake of unity, to honor the Other, and to place persons before positions. Only if you are free can you make of your encounter with another an invitation to freedom.

We might call this making of yourself a safe context for the Other the interior dimension of the We-They dynamic. The less 'safety,' or 'we-ness' exists in the particular form of your encounter with others, the more of this conscious we-building will be needed before meatier and more robust interactions are possible. The feeling of 'we-ness' can suddenly disappear if some unexpected difference-between-us comes to light. Were we getting along just fine until you said you are not like me in some aspect I depend upon for safety (You're not a vegetarian? You voted for WHOM?!?! You liked *that* book? You let your kids do what?!?!)?

---

[85] This is not permission to 'be condescending,' only to place yourself at his disposal, or to lift the Other 'above' yourself, per Philippians 2:3: "Let nothing be done through selfish ambition or conceit, but in lowliness of mind let each esteem others better than himself."

"Five times a second, at an unconscious level, your brain is scanning the environment around you and asking itself: Is it safe here or is it dangerous."[86] In a flash, a 'we' can become a 'we-they,' so be prepared and prayerful before stepping onto the holy ground of the presence of persons. Your structure and the structure of the form will help support your interior spaciousness from collapsing in fear when you feel betrayal, or suddenly 'not like' someone who is in your intimate circle.

**Structure – The Exterior Dimension**

I call the interior dimension 'with' strength, and the exterior dimension 'against' strength. When you have a strong, integrated sense of Self, and clarity about your boundary, identity, or definition, you are proof against a good bit of the reactive contraction fear can stimulate. You don't have to prove your rightness, power, or adequacy to anyone if you never feel it is threatened. 'Against' strength is demanding of us, and of our audience, or worthy opponents. It aims outward, expanding and defending territory, engaging in argument and verbal fencing. It's certainly not for everyone, or for every conversation, but it's the kind of strength that attracts others to build up their own skills.

External structural supports such as a clearly articulated form, the presence of rules, a facilitator, formal prayer for this form, excellent discussion questions, a great location, a time limit, formal courtesies, etc… combine with your own personal strengths to help open up a 'space' for harder,

---

[86] Michael Bungay Stanier, *The Coaching Habit: Say Less, Ask More & Change the Way You Lead Forever*, pg. 118

wider, more tense, less homogenous interaction. If you picture your own 'boundary' as an interface between your own interior freedom and the conversational context, then it's easy to see (analogically) that the boundary of each 'We' is an interface between the interior dimension, or we-ness, and the exterior dimension of the conversation-form we create together. That form allows some elements inside that provoke and challenge us to respond, while keeping out others.

The boundary of any form has, to some degree, this semi-permeability of structure. The Jews were given rules for the aliens in their midst; a cell wall keeps the sodium and potassium in balance between the interior and extracellular environments; the placenta receives toxins from Baby for disposal, while transmitting nutrients in small-enough packages; a tree pulls non-organic minerals from the soil and transforms them into living tissue and food; the seed opens out into an enormous seed-bearing structure; the clarity of Truth holds open space for loving, safe context.

Truth becomes substantial, building structure, which opens space filled with infrastructure that offers greater capacity to receive substance. Freedom *in* us is the degree to which we are in correspondence with factors of Realty (some are external/objective, some are internal/subjective, but freedom begins with this structural strength). Freedom *between* us depends upon the degree to which we are in unity with each other as persons. Woe to the 'we' that is powered only by 'against' strength. Without the coherence that only Love can provide, a 'We' becomes brittle and may crumble. Only Love can reconcile the tensions that threaten to unmake a 'We' and the interpersonal forms we create together. Because we bring Christ, we bring that

Love and that possibility of life-giving relationship to every interaction.

Imagine a continuum of affiliation from your most intimate 'We' to the impossible 'They'. The boundaries of each Self, or each 'We' form the full spectrum, bridging and connecting you even to the farthest-away 'They.' Love is moving back-and-forth all along that continuum of affiliation, through your freedom – weaving you together, ultimately, with those who are so alien, so not-you, so distant-in-time, or so threatening that you can barely see them. Love is able, in the largesse and courtesy of God, to proportion itself all along the spectrum, shaking and strengthening the structure that is You as it moves through your actual forms to Others.

**Reweaving the Context of Personhood**

Polarization is the rending of that continuum into two opposed poles, extremes, positions, camps, or ideologies where persons are trapped and unable to reweave the social fabric that supports the rising of free human beings. In this case, the 'way where there is no way'[87] is not a compromise between two erroneous, or incomplete positions, but a true *via media* where the road rises above the plane of division to the possibility of unity. The Way of Christ is the narrow road where only He can keep us, not a deliberately small place of deliverance for an inner ring with the password, secret handshake, or special knowledge.

---

[87] Isaiah 43:19: "Behold, I will do a new thing. Now it shall spring forth; Shall you not know it? I will even make a road in the wilderness and rivers in the desert."

A lack of vagal tone can leave people stranded in a constant, destructive, self-defense mode, with a narrow, objective perspective that prevents intimacy of persons. At the opposite extreme from the fight-or-flight response, they may be left collapsed and mired in a self-negating, or dissociated mode with little-to-no boundary of Self or capacity to engage with persons (social engagement – with Christ and the saints through prayer and Sacraments, and with the persons around us – is the number one way to restore our vagal equilibrium and flexibility). Just so, our lack of full-spectrum freedom of mobility along 'the whole' (or 'a growing section of,' or 'some extent of the whole') continuum of affiliation results in similar disengagement and rending of the social fabric. The Church, alone, as the Person of Christ, is truly able to span the actual whole spectrum of "all people, in all places, at all times" which corresponds to God's universal communication of Himself.

A healthy vagal tone promotes engagement-without-fear, or work-with-freedom-in-it. The SNS is activated by the will to act, and does not override the capacity to act freely. Granted, there are truly dangerous moments when it is highly desirable to simply react in quick self-defense. But to stay constantly in that state fractures and flattens the individual and his relationships. The same healthy vagal tone promotes parasympathetic relaxation, intimacy-without-fear, or capacity-for-persons. Granted, there are times we need complete rest from tension, stimulation, and social demands, and times when complete dorsal vagal collapse is a last-resort self-defense if we are faced with overwhelming opposition, or circumstances. But to remain isolated, disconnected, or floating in virtual worlds is a grave danger to the person and to the social forms he will not have strength to keep coherent.[88]

---

[88] See Charlotte Ostermann, *Upschooling*, Chapter 12 "Homeschooling to Rock the World" for more on 'flatitudes and floatitudes'.

The center, or high point in vagal tone and in social fabric is the possibility of play – an off-the-plane-of-tension, paradox-resolving point where work-and-rest, self-and-other, symbol-and-meaning rise to generate newness of life.[89]

**Are You With Me?**

Another way to visualize the continuum of affiliation is as a human ladder. In one of my family's stories, the rescue of someone at the bottom of a steep slope was accomplished by such a ladder: man after man after man, holding hands, and each holding one spot along that impossible slope so that others could get up and down holding those 'rungs' to bring up the injured. The people of God are, wherever they are located in space-time, or in some chain of affiliation, are something of a rescue structure within the world, helping the collapsing structures of the post-Christian world remain open to the Word, to the light, to the flow of grace and mercy by which Christ communicates Himself to them in Love.

Because He is – His Church is, we are – here, every human being stands in some relation to Him, and has some degree of connectedness to Him – to the Church, to you. The highest forms call other forms into comparison, into the light of their glory, or into judgment to some degree. There are forms so fearfully and wonderfully made – such as *persons*, Tolkien's *Lord of the Rings*, the works of Shakespeare, Bach and Mozart, the Liturgies of the Mass, or the Chartres Cathedral – that you judge them at peril

---

[89] See Charlotte Ostermann, *Souls at Play – Reflections on Creativity and Culture*

of being found wanting. The Church is, each of us is, and Christ is such a form.

As we turn 'in' toward our 'we-ness,' anyone who is not with us, here, is against us to some degree. We use 'differentiation' and 'against' strength to form verbal structures that make clear our boundary. Once those are strong, nuance, 'with' strength, and the infrastructure of rich interiority enter to weave us together, help us find commonality, keep us in unity with the adjacent 'They'. As we turn 'outward,' toward 'They,' we find grounds for solidarity in our common humanity, interests, organizational memberships, and in Christ's own words: "He who is not against me is for me."[90] We establish a context of unity, safety and love within which to form verbal structures of conformation, 'with' strength, and connection to one another. The content of Truth generates context, and the context of Love fills with content. The in-filling provides the inner richness and infrastructure that support our growing freedom, and the out-reaching provides the affordances and integrity of the external structure that increasingly embodies our love for others.

In conversation, we turn and turn again within the boundary of this small form until (hopefully) it has structural integrity to both resonate with Truth and shine with Love. Gradually, the form 'We' is given greater and greater verbal infrastructure by which to articulate and bear and delight in the diversity we find within. Gradually, the form 'We-They' produces greater and greater mediating structure by which to resolve tensions creatively and bring about the interpenetration of persons that makes the Church both a

---

[90] Luke 9:50: "Jesus said, "for whoever is not against you is for you."

ladder-that-leads-by-proportion to Christ, and a ladder-that-rescues-by-connection to Christ. Connectedness can be seen as 'horizontal,' and 'proportion' as a 'vertical' super-connectedness. Catholics communicate Christ, by thus raising up the free human person to resonate with the Word and to establish compound forms of unity which, likewise, resound Christ.

Chapter 6

# Rhetoric for the New Evangelization

In dialogue, someone is willing to exchange ideas with you. You create the formal context for that two-way exchange, and your intention to place human unity above results drapes the content in love. With rhetoric, you move a step further away from the person you hope to influence (you may be giving a speech, writing an article, or planning to speak to someone who is resistant to your message). That distance may tempt you to talk 'at' them, but your concern for them as persons fills the space with love – heart-hospitality – that helps you find a way your heart can speak to theirs. Here, you craft the content to be given without expectation of reciprocal exchange.

Aristotle's *Rhetoric* – the classical text on the subject of using words to persuade – may seem outdated in a world full of electronic communication, virtual conversations, memes and taglines. Once we see, however, that verbal skill (virtue, or power) is at the heart of what it means to be 'people of the Word,' then it's clear that rhetoric must have a significant connection to the communication of Christ.

I was surprised when a Rhetoric teacher at a Catholic college – asked if his students were becoming better able to persuade others toward the Faith – said, "They get 'Catholic' everywhere on this campus, but my class is secular. We don't use rhetoric in evangelization." Well, maybe we should! The Catechism agrees that we should, indeed, concern ourselves with *discovering the best means of persuasion.* "The initiative of lay Christians is necessary especially when the matter involves discovering or inventing the means for permeating social, political, and economic realities with the demands of Christian doctrine and life."[91]

Aristotle emphasized that rhetoric should be ordered to Truth. The Sophists of his day were more interested in displaying rhetorical power to persuade listeners or readers toward any-old position. Rhetoric aimed at articulating what is actually true was a big improvement. A Catholic rhetoric should be even more fully developed, at least (or, especially) when it comes to communicating Christ. If the Sophists were 'dots' positioned all over the map, and if Aristotle pulled them together into a line whose endpoint was Truth, what might we add?

**Structure is Form, Rising**

Christ added a point above the plane of two-dimensional contention, where the form of Truth can be seen to rise into its fullest dimensionality. Indeed, natural reason rose as far as it could, reaching for the infusion from beyond the natural plane toward the 'unknown god'. Christ condescended, in love, to meet man at this apex, where the heights of man's own power left him still helpless to effect real newness of life and reconciliation with God. His complete resurrection of the whole possibility of personhood, though predicated on the natural reality, far overshadowed it – much as He continues to overshadow

---

[91] *Catechism of the Catholic Church,* 899

hosts with His Real Presence. Rhetoric can 'rise' to offer the world 'three dimensional' verbal structures within which the skeletal structure of truth as argument can be encountered and appropriated, becoming infrastructural support for Truth within the hearer. In this sense, every truth well-told may help persuade recipients to resonate more fully with Truth.

Rhetoric concerned with the communication of Christ lays the strengths of its forms at the foot of the Cross, gives them through and in unity with the Church, and focuses less on techniques than on love for the persons receiving gifts in rhetorical forms. Catholic rhetoric needs also to find new forms that may not look like a thesis-controlled paper, or sound like a keynote speech, but that help communicate truth-in-love into flattened and darkened minds. St. Paul was definitely concerned with persuasive rhetoric, advising that "by all means" we should save, or rescue some.[92]

Until you believe that to be trapped within any thought system (narrative, form, ideology) built of, or bent by lies is a condition to be rescued *from*, all this persuading may seem to be meaningless word games. Hopefully, you've realized the stark differences between forms and structures that open to and resonate with truth, and those that don't. One is a playground, the other a prison; in one a symphony resounds and, in the other, the sounds of words being abused, losing their dignity, becoming divorced from reality, collapsing in impotence and turning man over to the enemies of his freedom. Josef Pieper connects abuse of language directly with the degradation of persons:

---

[92] 1 Corinthians 9:22: "To the weak I became as weak, that I might win the weak. I have become all things to all men, that I might by all means save some."

> ...the abuse of political power is fundamentally connected with the sophistic abuse of the word, indeed, finds in it the fertile soil in which to hide and grow and get ready, so much so that the latent potential of the totalitarian poison can be ascertained, as it were, by observing the symptom of the public abuse of language. The degradation, too, of many through man, alarmingly evident in the acts of physical violence...has its beginning, certainly much less alarmingly, at that almost imperceptible moment when the word loses its dignity. The dignity of the word...consists in this: through the word is accomplished...communication based on reality.[93]

Strongholds, structures built of lies, or 'bunkers' (as Pope Benedict XVI called them in his Regensburg Address)[94] are by nature self-referential forms without 'windows', or full correspondence to reality. Instead of resonating with and amplifying the sound of truth, they are threatened by truth as it shakes them to reveal structural flaws. Because they are verbal (books, policies and procedures, by-laws, journal articles, long marketing funnel stories, pamphlets, speeches, systematic theologies, etc...), and those inside may not have the verbal power to dismantle complex verbal structures, and because they have the strengths of truth twisted and verbal craftsmanship, these structures may be powerful traps. Because they grow into social systems that serve us to some degree (an education system, a medical system, a system of government or economics, a system

---

[93] Josef Pieper, *Abuse of Language Abuse of Power*, pg. 33
[94] Pope Benedict XVI, Lecture at Regensburg University, September 9, 2006

of organizational communication or distribution of goods, the penal system, for examples), verbal structures become almost impossible to overturn.

**Principles of Rhetoric**

Rhetoric begins at the level of the underlying words, or *logics* of social structures, not to bring violent revolution and destruction, but to shake and renew them with the *logos* of freedom. Any structure can benefit by the question, "Does this structure support and cultivate human freedom and integral human development?" and people of the Word can pose it.[95] A good question is a very tiny piece of rhetoric that provokes others to think, and to be interested in finding an answer. We'll look later at other new forms we may create to open the way for communication of Christ.

If we begin with the simplified definition of rhetoric as 'the art of finding the best possible means to persuade someone of truth,' then we can find ways to do this kind of persuading in our own forms to help rescue others from bent verbal structures. A course in Rhetoric can walk you through the many, many *means* identified by Aristotle of proving your point, teach you to link the best into a compelling proof-of-thesis speech, article, paper, or blog post, and offer various techniques to practice weaving into and around your thesis to give your thoughts greater 'carrying power'. It should also help you to identify when those techniques are being used to influence and manipulate you.

---

[95] See the encyclical *Caritas en Veritate* for more on integral human development.

Enormous funding supports research on effective (powerful) marketing and manipulation techniques that trace their origins to classical rhetoric, as used by the Sophists. Modern advertising campaigns are aided by the use of fMRI research to discover the means which best trigger specific neurological responses to imagery and text. Using pleasure, fear and aversion reactions, marketers craft messages that aim to bypass your logical, verbal reasoning to get your body (or your child) involved in pushing you toward certain products or choices. Choices made reactively are actually made in bondage. Unlike a choice made consciously, based on a good judgement, they contract, rather than expand, your freedom.

While we can appreciate the value of hospitality, the trustworthiness of many authority figures, the environmental impact of warm social engagement, and the good of associating our messages with images that evoke positive emotions, we will want our rhetoric to help others move toward *free* act – based less on emotion or dependence on other minds, and more on judgement and experiential validation of the proposal of truth. Whether the message, or atmosphere, is designed to trigger an emotional reaction, trust in experts, or peer pressure to conform, these sophistries are not invitations to freedom and not appropriate for the communication of Christ. Even if we could, somehow, design a message in a form that resulted in a knee-jerk 'choice to become Catholic,' we wouldn't want to. The Church has always understood that the process of conversion should not be compelled and, when authentic, is likely to proceed in slow, small steps taken in freedom.

**The Little Ways of Rhetoric**

In *The Journey to Truth is an Experience*, Fr. Giussani teaches us to take the time for a rhetoric of relationship that, while lovingly meeting a person where they are, desires – also in love – to reach toward his freedom from within our own, to elicit new awareness and provoke his own initiative.[96] We need, first, a clear definition of what we want to achieve. For example:

- I want to help him see that his negative view of Catholic teaching has come from a pastor who is hostile to the Faith and misinformed. I hope he will bring any questions he has to me for the actual answers.

- I want him to notice that the words and meditations of the Rosary are from Scripture, and agree not to speak of it as 'an abomination' any more.

- I want him to acknowledge that the Church is not in full unity, and that our divisions hurt the world… then pray with me for unity (*a la* John 17).

- I want him to become interested in the historical origin of the canon of Scripture and borrow my book to satisfy that curiosity.

- I want to cause some cognitive dissonance with his negative view of nuns by showing him a video of nuns having fun…just to plant a seed, not to lead to any specific act.

---

[96] Luigi Giussani, *The Journey to Truth is an Experience*

- I want him to notice that his drug use began in a deep neediness which drugs aren't satisfying. I'll suggest the real need is for God, and tell him our church is a safe, open space to pray or just to light a candle as a prayer…hoping he remembers that and goes in sometime soon.
- I hope his attraction to beauty will cause him to say yes to my concert invitation, even though it's sacred music.

Once we know what we want to achieve, we craft a simple, accurate verbal structure that makes no demands, but is, rather, an invitation to his freedom.

- "Sometimes people who are hostile to Catholicism are misinformed about it. I hope you'll let me help find authentic Catholic answers to your questions so you can compare your thoughts with the insider's perspective."
- "I love the words and images of the Rosary – straight from Scripture. It's painful to hear you call it an abomination. Would you be willing to stop using that phrase, just for me?"
- "You and I both see the Church as the Body of Christ and the answer to man's needs. If we can agree that divisions between us hurt Him and impede His message, we could pray together for unity. It doesn't have to mean that you or I convert immediately. Will you pray with me as Christ prayed in John 17, that we may be one?"

You won't in all likelihood get much of a chance in a sound-bite world to give a speech *a la* Aristotle. The world needs Catholic speakers, leaders, politicians, teachers, and influencers with training and skill in rhetoric. It also needs the little ways of persuasion, observation, questioning, nudging, provocation, witnessing and teaching that fit into interactions with friends, beggars, cashiers, co-workers, teammates, and service providers. The one builds entire thought structures (hopefully excellent ones that support and invite free action), and the other – Everyman's way – plants seeds that, hopefully, will open within an Other, provoking him to question, to validate a proposal of truth, to seek application in his own experience, to interest himself in learning more, to say yes to an invitation, or to notice when his act is more of a reaction than a free response.

To this end, the most important contribution classical Rhetoric makes to your communication of truth in love is the admonition to know your audience. How will you choose what means of persuasion will be most effective if you have no idea what motivates them, what they consider 'good,' 'valuable,' 'noble,' or 'pleasant'? In our day, we are drowning in a sea of 'communication.' Every surface, screen, story, sign, show and star has a message for us about what to do next, who is right, whom to trust, what button to click or product to buy. We've become inured to messages in self-defense, and impotent to pull out or to ponder meaning brought to us in the cacophony. 'Signal' is lost in the 'noise' of the surround-sound of more information than we can process. All of it has the characteristic of being broadcast, not to each of us personally, but to a demographic, a category, an average, a fan club, or a 'type'. Even when it is 'targeted' it has this impersonal quality of broadcast – literally, seed sown widely in the anticipation some will grow.

**Personal Encounter**

In real, personal relationships – even in the face-to-face exchange with a stranger – we have an opportunity to be heard in spite of all this noise. That opportunity, that new rhetoric, is communication with compassion. We can place ourselves in unity with the Other as an act of love – asking the Holy Spirit to establish a connection of persons which does not depend upon mutuality. The Other needn't love us. We love, because God first loved us.[97] His love – perhaps long-ignored and unrequited – made it possible for us to love Him, so now we can open a way of love. We have freedom to place ourselves in relationship, into a unity that invites the participation of the Spirit, with another person in a loving way, even if for a brief moment. We might call this a 'rhetoric of unity,' which looks not to win arguments, but to communicate Christ by the best possible means, offered in love through our freedom. "The sharing is done through the Spirit, the *Ruah* or breath of the Father that carries the Word. The breath is the atmosphere, the conversation, the kiss by which the two are united in giving and receiving. …The Spirit is the Rhetoric of God."[98] Stratford Caldecott continues:

> *Heart Speaks Unto Heart.* This motto of the Blessed John Henry Newman, adopted from St. Francis de Sales, contains the essence of a 'philosophy of communication,' which is also a philosophy of education.[99] …every person has an interior life that cannot be divulged except by deliberately 'opening up' the heart, and allowing the life that is within it to flow through words and gestures into the other

---

[97] 1 John 4:19: "We love, because He first loved us."
[98] Stratford Caldecott, *Beauty in the Word*, pg. 16
[99] Stratford Caldecott, *Beauty in the Word*, pg. 84

> person.[100] ...under the heading of 'Rhetoric,' ...I am discussing the dimension of education that concerns interpersonal communication, or the creation and sustaining of a community and a tradition. Here what we are by our actions is the foundation of everything else. You cannot communicate a truth that has not changed you. You cannot *build a community* on a truth that has not been incorporated into you.[101]

Here, Caldecott has touched the heart of this book: communication partakes of the art of teaching, is a kind of education that involves life-to-life transfer instead of mere information transfer, and depends upon the wholeness, integrity and freedom of persons in community to voice the 'rhetoric of God'. You're actually preparing others for Christ when you 'teach' them who they are as human persons, by treating them with courtesy. Evangelization is not only telling the good news that Christ *is*, but also the good news that each person actually *is*, in your eyes, a communication from God.

To place myself in your position, outside my 'we,' and to walk you gently 'in' toward mine is (as Balthasar teaches in *Convergences*) the key to communicating Christ. 'Truth' in 'Love' is Christ – carried in a word, act, gesture, or art form – in the power of the Holy Spirit. This is, compared to a rhetoric of apologetics and of argument, a rhetoric of *being*, of seed-planting, of small companionship and small steps. Though Dialectic – learning to argue logically with skill – precedes Rhetoric in the classical Trivium, I have left Argument for later in this book. We need loving, compassionate, personal interest in the smallest, most

---

[100] Stratford Caldecott, *Beauty in the Word*, pg. 85
[101] Stratford Caldecott, *Beauty in the Word*, pg. 86

communicable, seed-like means of persuasion – best for a particular, actual person – before we take on the project of evangelization through larger verbal and gestural structures, or compound forms.

Seeds are forms that carry their own 'energy of expansion' into deeply packed soil where, we hope, they may open. The small word-forms, gestures, persuasive messages you give may become living structure within another person. In the context of small, everyday, interpersonal exchanges, your words are less likely to be about God than about the things of everyday life. You'll communicate Christ every time you affirm the humanity and dignity of another person ("Thank you for keeping these bathrooms so nice for all of us!" "Your beautiful smile might be the only one some customers see all day...keep it up!" "You handled my complaint with such compassion." "It sounds like you're having a hard day...I'll pray for you.").

**Love Comes First**

Before you exercise your 'against' strength, develop the interior dimension of communication – skill and practice in establishing unity, prayerful and loving concern for others, capacity to be fully present to and affected by persons – which provides 'core' strength for further 'extension' across wider 'We-They' territory and into the culture. You should find yourself growing in the integration of 'with' and 'against' strength as you rise up in skill, maturity, and freedom. 'With' strength is a more maternal, homely, feminine counterpart to the masculine, external-facing, enemy-defeating strength that is also needed in a hostile world. Yet Christ Himself has spoken of its priority in communicating Him. Love is the without-which-zero communication of Christ is possible and must be extended even to our enemies if we would prioritize the souls of persons above our positions in an argument.[102]

Until you can love, practice your 'against' strength in resistance to the manipulation and lies all around you. Try out your arguments against parents, teachers and friends who play 'devil's advocate'. Structure your intellect to resonate with truth and against lies by reading and studying the excellent rhetoric of trustworthy influencers. Your life is, in itself, an argument. Every choice you make argues for others to make that choice and to choose against other options – even if those choices are trivial. As you grow more strongly 'for' more important 'messages,' you need to own those messages more deeply, because they will bring you into tension, into conflict with others. Before you can reason with others, reasonable trust must be worked into your own moral, spiritual and intellectual fiber, or 'structure,' so that you become a context of reason. Just as trust is the basis of reason, a rhetoric of unity is the basis for a rhetoric of argument. Reason and argument will often reach the limit of your natural strength, but Love never fails to go beyond it.

What you stand for becomes a form standing against everything else. He, for whom you stand, rises up through you as a stumbling block, against anyone who is not for Him.[103]

---

[102] 1 Corinthians 13:1: "Though I speak with the tongues of men and of angels, but have not love, I have become sounding brass or a clanging cymbal."

[103] Matthew 12:30: "The one who is not with Me is against Me; and the one who does not gather with Me scatters."

Chapter 7

# Evangelization as Argument

Rhetoric extends from the classical classroom to the news media, the world of advertisement and entertainment, the practice of law, the arts of teaching and speechmaking, and into the political sphere. Communicating Christ, though, is a more focused application for conversational, dialogical, and rhetorical techniques and principles. That focus is evangelization. The ultimate aim of communicating Christ, and the Good News about His gift of Presence, is to win others over – for their sakes – to acceptance of the gift of Faith.

The Catholic model for communication developed so far takes us from intimacy, through tension, into community and ever-wider we-they gaps to build bridges, indicate paths to unity, and keep peace. It weaves together the interior dimension of the power of love and the exterior dimension of the power of skill training and practice in words – by way of the person doing the work – who becomes 'woven together,' 'well-integrated,' or 'free' in the process. It builds, first, a core strength of deep integration with family, then community, and then a growing extension strength of Self, acting to integrate others into the encounter with Christ, into the Church, and into the structure of Truth. It seeks not only to communicate about Christ, but to give Him in actuality through the gift of Self.

For this, a free human person is needed. He is generated by the Christ-life within him as it is drawn up and forward through the demands of building community, resolving tension creatively, and offering unity to those with whom he has less and less in common. Those demands are impossible for him to meet without supernatural assistance. The sooner he realizes that, the better, because the entrance of Love into the 'equation' of conversing, dialoguing, arguing, (and, later, making new forms) dwarfs his rightness, his skills, and his power.

The one who loves much is the one ready and able – whatever his training, or skill level – to communicate Christ. He is, in fact, only able to love much because Christ is present, initiating the flow. That he does love much indicates that he is free. The real task of evangelization is to remain free – an open channel for the Love who communicates Christ, and His invitation to freedom. This is why a child, or an uneducated saint may be the best evangelist. This is why being *in* love – in communion with, dwelling richly with, deeply rested by, set free by Christ – gives your communication the power, or impetus of love to carry your forms deeply into small people, dark places, hostile territory, and hard realities.

So, we come to the 'against' strength of argument with the caution that, without love, it will be a clashing cymbal – one more noise in a noisy world. It may accomplish its own purposes, but not Christ's.

**Apologetics is a Form of Argument**

If you're excited about the Faith, you get excited by the chance to argue its merits. Do you love the Other(s)?

Have you stopped to pray for him/them and for the Spirit's help with this conversation? Can you accurately – to his satisfaction – state the position of the Other? Have you validated the proposal of truth in your own actual experience? Are you in a state of grace? Do you have a sense of what motivates the Other, what he thinks will bring him happiness or pleasure, what he has already substituted for the life of Christ to fill his need for reconciliation with God?

Do you have any understanding of what material has built his structure so far – trauma, literature, influencers, news media, friends, education, etc…, etc…? Do you realize that this structure may be threatened, and that you may seem threatening, if you challenge some part of it? Have you taken steps to build trust, create a warm and safe context, show he can disagree without losing your love, and engage with him as an actual person (not as a label, an abstraction, or a member of a category)? Are you clear about what one small step you want to persuade him to take, or what question you want him to answer for himself? Are you prepared to love him if he doesn't accept your invitation to freedom? Is the unity between you more important than 'winning' a conversation, or a conversion?

Well then, charge ahead! Otherwise, keep practicing, keep getting to know him, keep saying yes to God's invitations to freedom. Not everyone is ready for the demands of good argument.

Apologetics is, Balthasar said, one face of theology. The first is a contemplation, directed toward God, of the revelation or events of salvation – immersion in prayer and adoration. The second is the proclamation of the Church, in which the Spirit translates her witness of God's act of salvation into universal forms for every nation, or people, to receive. The second is communication, from inside the Church to outsiders. The third is the 'apologetic theology,' or 'dialogical theology' which "leads step by step, in conversation with the brother, from outside to inside". The Christian "can open to the Lord the other person's final otherness in being and thinking, no longer through words and arguments, but through…a silent, accompanying witness." "Thus the three forms of theology form a system of circulation. Or rather, it is the same face in three-fold, changing expression."[104]

Dialogue with someone outside the Faith is a particular form – a 'we-they' – that calls upon the content of our beliefs. Not all dialogue involves apologetics, nor does all communication of Christ involve the content of Faith. When, in dialogue, our goal is to witness to the Faith and accompany an Other as he moves toward it, our apologetics will be 'dialogic,' and take the perspective of finding and building upon common ground, a way we might both move toward higher ground, or building a bridge to articulate and help resolve the tension between us. A good bridge will also bear the 'compression' of our walking back and forth over it together. If he then does not budge, it is not fair to say he has rejected Jesus, or rejected the Faith. Truth is objective, but is conveyed subjectively – through persons. He may reject not so much the Truth, but the instrument. And he may, as well, not want to reject the person communicating, even as he remains unconvinced to shift his position. So, don't condemn him, or take his position as a personal rejection.

---

[104] Hans Urs von Balthasar, *Convergences*, pg. 65, 66

### Dialogic Apologetics is an Art

Apologetics – being ready and able to "give an answer" for your beliefs – is a form of rhetoric, or argument, that requires intellectual preparation and practice with the content of your reasons for belief. Conversation and dialogue is less about 'content' than 'context'. Relational context – mutual understanding, trust, life experienced together over time – is built of content you already share, such as interests, mutual friends, beliefs in common, and experience in contexts that you share, such as workplace and family.

'Dialogic apologetics' implies a middle ground that is at once 'less than' formal apologetics and 'more than' simple conversation. It implies an intentionality, or desire to infuse conversation with Catholic content – for the good of the non-Catholic, and in the spirit of gifting him with blessings – but stops short of a utilitarian abuse of the friendship as a dumping ground for everything you learn in Apologetics class. As the artist struggles to bring Idea into Form without violating either the ideal or the material, through obedience to the principles of artistic excellence, so the dialogic apologist struggles to reduce all the intellectual content of apologetics into words that may help communicate with the Other not just reasons for belief, but real encounter with Christ. He must speak the truth, but in the context of a love that has real interest in the other person, real humility and vulnerability before him, real concern with his eternal soul and spiritual well-being.

We need a dialogue to establish common ground before we know what persuasion, or argument is needed. "…modern sceptics always begin by telling us what they do not believe. But even in a sceptic we want to know first what he does believe. Before arguing, we want to know what we need not argue about," says G.K. Chesterton. He goes on to offer four things, which he calls the "four sanities," that "all sane men do believe in," "leaving religion for the moment wholly out of the question". We can all agree that:

1. the world around [us] and the people in it are real, and not [our] own delusion or dream.

2. this world not only exists, but matters, and that we have some obligation …to interest ourselves in this vision or panorama of life.

3. there is such a thing as a self, or ego, which is continuous.

4. we have a power of choice and responsibility for action.[105]

Dialogic apologetics is an art that can be modeled, but must be learned in practice. You'll give words – forms you create, verbal structures made of the 'material' of literary allusion, history, quotations, life stories, images, etc.… You – the person, the apologist, the artist, the friend – are the 'womb' to those forms – where they are draped in the qualities of your integrity, passion, and love. In a sense, your heart is 'womb' to the person listening, extended into the space-between-you as a place where you are knitted together by the Spirit who offers encounter with Christ. In the next chapter, we'll look at engaging his imagination to help him extend, or open his boundary toward you.

---

[105] *Philosophy for the Schoolroom*, G.K. Chesterton

**When Do We Argue?**

Conversation is not a contest, and not a debate. In Dialogue, we exercise 'with' strength more than 'against' strength, to find common ground. By the use of Rhetoric, we seek to engage him 'where he is,' and bring him with us, point by point, persuasively, toward our position. Even in Apologetics – a form of argument – we take a dialogical, or 'with' approach, more often than not. Especially if you're fond of a robust argument, you may be wondering, is there a place for argumentation in evangelization?

Certainly argument has contributed to the structural strength of the Church. The canon of Scripture, the Doctrines of the Faith, the *Summa Theologiae* of St. Thomas Aquinas, her teachings on social justice and human dignity, and the *Catechism of the Catholic Church* were all derived through skilled argumentation, for just a few examples. Chesterton (whose own *Heretics* is another example of 'against' strength that builds up and protects the faithful) wrote, "I know many people will tell you that nothing has ever come out of arguments; and I tell you that everything has always come out of arguments."

Unless you are on a debate team, in a Socratic dialogue, or School of Law, you may be discouraged from the taking and defending of positions. In other contexts, there is less willingness to bear the tensions of argument. Gerald Graff, looking into "how schooling obscures the life of the mind," observes

> For many students, the very word 'argument' (like 'criticism') conjures up an image not of spirited conversational give and take, but of acrimonious

> warfare in which competitors revile each other and make enemies yet rarely change each other's minds. Disputes end up producing winners and losers or a stalemate that frustrates all parties; either way they are useless except for stirring up bad blood. This tendency to equate persuasion with aggression is especially rife among students who grow up in liberal pluralist surroundings, where 'Live and let live' is a ruling maxim and 'whatever' the popular mantra.[106]

> ...much of the oft-lamented relativism of today's youth actually stems from the difficulty of imagining a world in which their arguments would make a difference.[107]

Once students are let in on the secret that most influential intellectual work...springs from having something to contest, they can proceed with a clearer sense of their task.[108]

Besides poor education, other factors discourage us from engaging in argument.

**Why Not Argue?**

We tend not to argue because we lack common ground, we have no time for it, we are unable to articulate our own position well, or we fear losing (or losing confidence in our own position). Let's address those one at a time, then turn to some benefits of argument and suggestions for doing it well.

---

[106] Gerald Graff, *Clueless in Academe: How Schooling Obscures the Life of the Mind*, pg. 56
[107] Gerald Graff, *Clueless in Academe: How Schooling Obscures the Life of the Mind*, pg. 73
[108] Gerald Graff, *Clueless in Academe: How Schooling Obscures the Life of the Mind*, pg. 91

**Arguments Seem so…Argumentative**

The worst arguments may turn acrimonious, but the best are characterized by courtesy. In fact, the farther apart 'we' are from 'them,' the more important ground rules, taboos, and mutual assurance of respectful listening become. For example, the formal rules for debate, or *Robert's Rules of Order* can keep an argument from derailing into personal attack or tangential matter. The answer to awful arguments isn't to ban argument itself, or a person, or a topic, but to back up from the argument to discuss good, civil argument practices. Say "Yes, I will argue with you," to anyone who asks, and add, "but of course we must first discuss time and place, rules and taboos, topic and key definitions, time limits for each of our parts, whether this will be public or private, whether any particular sources of proof will be banned or required, whether an independent mediator is needed, who goes first, and what common ground we may take as given."

These preliminaries are not attempts to buy time (though the time involved may help cool heads and build relationship before argument begins), but real provisions for a good, civil argument. If at any point the preparations for argument become, themselves, contentious, the parties may need to admit that real argument has thus been proved untenable. The assertion that a heated disagreement should be settled "here and now!" (thus ruining the party, shutting others out of the conversation, etc…) is a lie. Retain your freedom to negotiate the terms of an argument, and to say no to it if terms can't be reached, or are breached.

**We Have Zero Common Ground**

False. Your desire to understand an opponent's position is common ground with him, as is your goodwill toward him and the intentional unity by which you make love the context for your contest. You surely will find some mutuality of goals and values – the four sanities, honesty, freedom, honoring parents, obeying laws, generosity, helping those in need, and being kind to others are all widely agreed upon. You should find common ground as you clarify what is actually to be argued about. You might agree on ends, or outcomes, but disagree on the means to accomplish them (making the *means* the topic to be argued, because the 'end' is now a given). You might agree to an action the other suggests, but point out that there are impediments making it impossible, or ways to improve its effectiveness. You might both disagree with a third party about the issue. You might agree that one of you will take the opposite position as strongly as possible, for the sake of a good argument. Inability to get to common ground comes from lack of clarity in knowing what you think, and why.


**We Haven't Got Time, It's a Pain**

We actually don't have time to argue about every little thing. We don't have to (and it would be unwise to try to) base every action on reasoned argument. Someone might argue that your 'quirks' and 'habits' are unreasonable, but it wouldn't be reasonable to stop life to argue about such petty matter. Choose the highest things, and those about which you are passionate or well-educated, and make time for an argument once you have a willing opponent.

**I Can't Say What I Mean**

Even if you never speak aloud, you should practice making clear to yourself whatever arguments you are living by. Write your own Credo to start. What do you believe, and why? Start in writing, for practice, or start in intimate conversation to hear for yourself what needs to be clarified, researched, learned, or otherwise improved. Clear writing supports any speaking you do. It originates in and leads to clear thinking. If you can submit your writing to someone for written critique and comment, you'll get the benefit of "iron sharpening iron" with some distance in time and space for processing the criticism without the embarrassment of being face-to-face. Reading excellent rhetoric and reproducing it in your own words is another great exercise. You in-form yourself with their excellent arguments, and strengthen your structure as you practice expressing the forms through your own 'material.'

**Fear of Failure**

If you never argue, you lose the chance to 'fail forward,' to learn from the strength of others where your weaknesses lie. Your arguments, won or lost, don't change the fundamental truths that you're arguing about. You may feel you've let down your 'side' if your argument goes poorly and the opponent remains unconvinced, convinces listeners he is right, or just makes you look and feel stupid and wrong. But who loses if you don't argue at all? If Truth is not communicated, it is silenced as effectively as if you didn't believe it. Truth has nothing to fear from error, and cannot be shaken. You, however, may need to admit you've got growing and learning to do, which is another 'win' for 'our team'. Get the help, the modeling, the class, the critique, or the practice you need, and get back in that ring. Or, spend more time in good conversation and reading to build up your strength in case, someday, you decide to argue again.

**'Against' Strength is Hard to Wield**

Finally, we come to the more external, 'against' nature of argumentation. All the 'Why Nots' come into play somewhere along the continuum from home, through Church, to public square, silencing and polarizing people who should be reasoning together. Voices, silenced, are gaps in the social fabric. Unless we take a new approach, we can't use argument – done well – to weave back together those unbridgeable gaps. There are times, as Coventry Patmore says, for being and speaking against:

> Toleration…may be a very one-sided bargain. It will not do to let falsehood and moral idiocy say to truth and honesty, "I will tolerate you, if you will tolerate me." There are truths which to many are incapable of proof, yet their denial is not to be tolerated, as the most tolerant society finds out when it is compelled to face the practical results of such denial. There are not 'two sides to every question,' nor, indeed, to any. Nor can you convert men to truth by seeming to meet them half-way. The most powerful solvent is the sharpest opposite. You can best move this world by standing and making it clear that you stand upon another.[109]

---

[109] Coventry Patmore

Timothy Gordon, in *Rules for Retrogrades*, suggests principles for the appropriate application of this sort of defense-of-the-Church, defense-of-the-home, defense-of-civil-society-and-freedom argumentation that is most decidedly needed in our day. He admits that the rescue mission he envisions is not for the faint of heart. I am cheered by the possibility that someone will even try to confront the systems of death and darkness, stupidity and silence, abuse of language and overt evil that Gordon's 'retrograde,' 'polymath,' 'God spies' war against with wit, honesty, skill and boldness. I hope he's raising a capable army that will "mobilize the English language and send it into battle."[110]

'Against' strength is a 'tough love' as practiced by Gordon's rules. On every page, I have written "Amen!" and "YES!" and also "But also…" and "And yet…". Gordon gets it: "…the good guys should err on the side of feistiness and fustiness with foes; they should err on the side of friendliness and fellow-feeling with friends."[111] He understands that any conversation can be framed by its 'we-ness' or its 'we-they' tensions, and gives his rules especially for use when 'they' are setting themselves up against reality, family, religion, life, truth, and freedom. A 'we-facing' counterpoint to his book would add a more feminine, subjective dimension, which is consonant with Gordon's sense that the two exist in a geometric proportion that keeps them in dynamic tension.

---

[110] The response of journalist Edward R. Murrow to Churchill's "We shall fight on the beaches" speech.
[111] Timothy Gordon, *Rules for Retrogrades*, pg. 65

Bishop Robert Barron, widely appreciated for his willingness to engage conversationally even with proponents of error, in his evangelistic zeal, advises a Thomistic approach to such potentially heated exchanges. Though St. Thomas disagreed with others, he was "more than willing to listen to them…to take their arguments seriously." The method begins with a clear statement of the issue, or disputed question. "Thomas then entertains a series of objections to the position that he will eventually take." He "presents these objections in their most convincing form." Finally, he "offers his own magisterial resolution of the matter" before answering each of the objections. His technique for refuting them "is to find something right in the objector's position and to use that to correct what he deems to be errant in it."[112] When truth comprehends error, love helps error find the way back.

This approach informs the Catholic Approach to Error suggested in Chapter 10 – In Conversation with Culture, as a way of preparing each other in 'we' conversations for more challenging 'we-they' dialogue and argument.

### Benefits of Training in Argument

Equipping the faithful to discern and be proof against the persuasive power of advertisements, marketing funnel stories, and propaganda is, perhaps, the most pressing reason for training in rhetoric and argumentation. Our own intellects will be strengthened by the exercise. Fr. Schall agrees:

---

[112] Bishop Robert Barron, "Thomas Aquinas and the Art of Making a Public Argument," National Catholic Register, July 10, 2016, Pg. 11

> Great thinkers, no doubt, can be and have been in error; Aristotle… understood that the knowledge of error – even great error – is not something that we should reject knowing. It is part of being free. …The history of error, the history of heresy, is as much a part of liberal education as is the history of truth. … Unless we understand the arguments against truth, we do not fully understand truth itself.[113]

If we can bear a few sparks, we'll gain the "iron sharpening iron" benefits of minds set 'against' one another in love. Finally, if we can gain enough confidence in the power of argument to do real good in the Church, the organization, the public sphere, we can boldly and lovingly undermine 'bent' structures, or persons, and set them on the path of robust, actionable verbal structures, toward truth and structural integrity. This re-form is needed, to some degree, by every person you know, every organization you're in, and every system that functions as a super-structure for your life. Argument might help it happen.

---

[113] James Schall, *Life of the Mind*, pg. 40

Chapter 8

# The Arts of Communication

St. Thomas Aquinas called his monumental body of writing 'straw'. Most of the work of J. R. R. Tolkien is a hidden iceberg his fans will never read. Many won't ever even read *Lord of the Rings*, thinking that seeing the movie is enough. Shakespeare did the hard lifting for modern derivatives with no gravitas and no attribution. Jane Austen's works are now the stuff of zombie parodies. Kansas Supreme Court Justice Caleb Stegall wrote over thirty pages of reasoned argument and legal history in rebuttal to the nonsensical majority opinion that the state constitution protected a 'right' to abortion. Few will ever read it, and fewer still with a willingness to change their minds. Masterworks of polyphony were lost in fires, beautiful craftsmanship lies hidden in cathedral nooks, and for every artist who gets attention hundreds die barely noticed.

So what's the good news? If you're an artist, you'll need to be offering your work without any interior demand for results – making form in freedom. If you're not an 'artist', you are still a 'maker,' with creative power to place meaning into form – in freedom. Art matters. It is, in fact, the mattering-forth-in-form (words, paint, music, film, stone) by which man's self-expression fills the world with law, beauty, institutions, inventions, and other evidence that man was made in the image of a creator.

All that 'straw' becomes the content filling the context we call 'culture'. We'll look at many of those forms of cultural content in later chapters. That which is true, good, and beautiful lends its strength to a culture of life and that which is bent, broken, and evil lends the strength of human intelligence to a culture of death. Our works will inevitably bear some of our own imperfection, but we have every hope that they will be woven together for good by the One to whom they are offered in worship.

The arts are powerful 'messaging systems,' because they are forms that take shape in the midst of tension. These forms are resolutions of tension – little responses to the encounter with reality, which re-present both the external, objective reality and the affective, subjective form that takes place within the one responding (the *instress* of reality, as Gerard Manley Hopkins would say). They, through the human person, are small fractals, examples, practice fields, vessels of creative intrusion into reality. The shape of the dynamic of art-making is the shape of the dynamic of creativity, and also the shape of the Holy Spirit's own creative, intrusive, surprising action in the world. God's response to the reality you encounter comes through you.

**Art Informs Communication**

For our Catholic model of communication, we've moved beyond the mere utterance of words, and beyond the science of transmitting them more effectively, to the wisdom of not communicating at all *unless* (or, communicating more 'three-dimensionally' *because*) we and our forms are vessels of Love's power to communicate

Himself. Communication becomes an 'art' when it is a conscious participation in something beyond ourselves, possesses a spark of divine power, and demands the integral development of the artist, as well as integrity in the forms he makes. Thus, we have considered the Art of Conversation ordered to building up community, the Art of Dialogue ordered to reweaving the social fabric, the Art of Rhetoric ordered to evangelization, and the Art of Argument that aims to set men free, or to build up and protect that freedom, or "correspondence to reality".[114]

Those might be considered the action-oriented, or external-facing forms of communication. C.S. Lewis wrote, "… in Rhetoric imagination is present for the sake of passion (and, therefore, in the long run, for the sake of action), while in poetry passion is present for the sake of the imagination, and therefore, in the long run, for the sake of wisdom or spiritual health – the rightness and richness of a man's total response to the world.[115] In the classical model of education, Poetics – creating verbal structures – follows Rhetoric as a way of persuading others not of a particular position, but into the lived experience of another's perspective, his imaginative world, or his encounter with reality. *Poiesis*, then, might be considered the interior-facing, *being*-oriented aspect of communication. It has to do with the making and self-giving of the maker, not only with his message.

By the placing of himself into the forms he creates, a maker receives himself back from them, whether an audience ever responds, or not. *Poiesis* (making, creating) is a fundamentally human capacity, not reserved to artists, and

---

[114] Fr. Luigi Giussani: "Freedom is the correspondence to reality, in the totality of its factors."

[115] C.S. Lewis, *A Preface to Paradise Lost*, pg. 53

one which forms in us, ultimately, a greater capacity for the reality we re-present. Catholic communicators – makers of form, people of word, artists of truth – are participating in the work of their own becoming. Made by a Creator, we clearly do not make ourselves, but as conscious 'material' are given the power to co-operate as willing clay with the work of the Potter.[116] And what is your will but the impetus to act, to do, to speak, to make – to enact the word "Amen" to the Father's "Let there be You"? As we speak of art forms, keep in mind that all form-making rises to become 'art' with the infusion of love made possible by your freedom in Christ.

Art forms offer a way of beauty that is a gentle context, inviting receptivity and engagement of the recipient's emotions and imagination. The metaphor given through words helps the listener hop up onto the ladder of proportion, by which he can see higher things analogically. The juxtaposition of visual or aural figures can move him – have the power to destabilize – causing a listener or viewer, even momentarily, to lose the security of Self-as-center that locks him into the prison of the imploding Self-without-Christ. "An encounter with the deeply beautiful… is a meeting that concerns and shakes the subject."[117] Your setting or characters may welcome readers into an experience of wonder that leads to philosophy, or a new human perspective that leads to empathy.

Works of beauty can be non-confrontational invitations to freedom, reminders of human dignity, and seeds of longing that awaken desire for transcendence in those who receive. The Catholic artist invites the Spirit to move upon the

---

[116] Isaiah 64:8: "You, Lord, are our Father. We are the clay, you are the potter; we are all the work of your hand."

[117] Bishop Robert Barron, *And Now I See*, pg. 89

forms he creates in resolution of tension, as a person might play a note upon a tensed violin string, or blow a tune through the form of a flute.

Holly Ordway, in *Apologetics and the Christian Imagination*, suggests we communicators of Christ aim for an approach that integrates reason and imagination:

> Certainly, there will always be some people who are most readily helped by apologetics that are based only in philosophical arguments or scriptural claims, or most immediately reached by evangelization that is purely emotional in its attraction. The Holy Spirit is not limited by our limitations. But this does not relieve us of the responsibility to do all that we can with what God has given us, to guide people to knowledge and love of Christ. An integrated approach to apologetics, one that makes good use of both reason and imagination, will help us greatly.[118]

We have mixed feelings about art. On the one hand, some see the arts as means for a completely non-confrontational invitation to the world we inhabit with Christ – a world in-formed by Sacrament, eternity, and transcendence. On the other hand are Catholics who are (understandably) wary of the arts and of artists, but who grudgingly acknowledge a role for art as a useful way of making our points about Christ. Somewhere between the making of emotional 'atmospheres' – contexts with no content – and the making of forms without interiority – content without context, truth without love – lies the possibility of well-integrated forms.

---

[118] Holly Ordway, *Apologetics and the Christian Imagination*, pg. 168

**Art is not Propaganda**

In *The Responsibility of the Artist,* Jacques Maritain addresses a common misunderstanding that the artist must be free from the imposition of all rules and expectations in order to reach excellence in his field. He emphasizes the superiority of the moral law, even above the sovereign prerogatives of the laws of Art.

> The highest moral virtues can never make up for the lack or mediocrity of the virtue of art. But it is clear that laziness, cowardice or self-complacency, which are moral vices, are a bad soil for the exercise of artistic activity. The moral constitution of the human subject has some kind of indirect impact on his art. ... A moral poison which warps in the long run the power of vision will finally, through an indirect repercussion, warp artistic creativity -- though perhaps this poison will have stimulated or sensitized it for a time. At long last the work always *avows*. When it is a question of great poets, this kind of avowal does not prevent the work from being great and treasurable, yet it points to some soft spot in this greatness. Furthermore, are not the inner inclinations of the artist the very channel through which things are revealed to him? Is it not in and through himself, through his own emotion and subjectivity, that the poet, in so far as poetic intuition is concerned, knows everything he knows? What is most real in the world thus escapes the notice of a darkened soul. [119]

---

[119] Jacques Maritain, *The Responsibility of the Artist,* Chapter IV- Poetry and Perfection of Human Life, https://maritain.nd.edu/jmc/etext/resart4.htm

The artist, or communicator, who would communicate Christ has the extra tension between virtue in the moral sphere and virtue in the domain of art to resolve in his forms. A conversation, or a novel can be violated by being used as a vehicle for a Moral Lesson. Excellent conversations and novels – those true to the ideals for art in that medium – may be filled with moral lessons, but those lessons are not 'the point.' Flannery O'Connor is famous for counseling artists not to turn out propaganda, and for enduring readers who just didn't see 'the point' of her stories.

> Every day we see people who are busy distorting their talents in order to enhance their popularity or to make money that they could do without. We can safely say that this, if done consciously, is reprehensible. But even oftener, I think, we see people distorting their talents in the name of God for reasons that they think are good – to reform or to teach or to lead people to the Church. And it is much less easy to say that this is reprehensible. ... The novelist who deliberately misuses his talent for some good purpose may be committing no sin, but he is certainly committing a grave inconsistency, for he is trying to reflect God with what amounts to a practical untruth.[120]

**Art is a Universal Calling**

St. Pope John Paul II, in his famous address to artists, considered that within and outside the Church, artists are influenced toward distortions in their understanding of their work. Likewise, makers who may not consider

---

[120] Flannery O'Connor, *Mystery and Manners*, pg. 174

themselves artists at all are deeply influenced in their consideration of whatever forms – words, gestures, events, institutions – they create. Denial, or distortion of the Imago Dei, and misunderstanding of the human person are expressed everywhere in today's cultures. Those cultures, then, of course, exert pressure upon man to take on the misshapen form.

> Not all are called to be artists in the specific sense of the term. Yet, as Genesis has it, all men and women are entrusted with the task of crafting their own life: in a certain sense, they are to make of it a work of art, a masterpiece. It is important to recognize the distinction, but also the connection, between these two aspects of human activity. The distinction is clear. It is one thing for human beings to be the authors of their own acts, with responsibility for their moral value; it is another to be an artist, able, that is, to respond to the demands of art and faithfully to accept art's specific dictates. This is what makes the artist capable of producing objects, but it says nothing as yet of his moral character. We are speaking not of moulding oneself, of forming one's own personality, but simply of actualizing one's productive capacities, giving aesthetic form to ideas conceived in the mind.
>
> The distinction between the moral and artistic aspects is fundamental, but no less important is the connection between them. Each conditions the other in a profound way. In producing a work, artists express themselves to the point where their work becomes a unique disclosure of their own

being, of what they are and of how they are what they are. And there are endless examples of this in human history. In shaping a masterpiece, the artist not only summons his work into being, but also in some way reveals his own personality by means of it. For him art offers both a new dimension and an exceptional mode of expression for his spiritual growth. Through his works, the artist speaks to others and communicates with them. The history of art, therefore, is not only a story of works produced but also a story of men and women. Works of art speak of their authors; they enable us to know their inner life, and they reveal the original contribution which artists offer to the history of culture.[121]

The *Letter to Artists* is of importance to artists and non-artists alike, who would restore to culture the image of God-the-artist whose human form bears his image to the world. Communicating Christ must be a work of art, because it is a work of Love. People of the Word are, thus, artists, and should appropriate counsel given for artists for the good of whatever creative making they do with the materials they are given.

> Every genuine inspiration, however, contains some tremor of that "breath" with which the Creator Spirit suffused the work of creation from the very beginning. Overseeing the mysterious laws governing the universe, the divine breath of the Creator Spirit reaches out to human genius and stirs its creative power. He touches it with a kind of inner illumination which brings together the sense of the good and the beautiful, and he awakens energies of

---

[121] St. Pope John Paul II, *Letter to Artists*, pg. 2

mind and heart which enable it to conceive an idea and give it form....[122]

St. Pope John Paul spoke specifically to artists, but I would hope for you to see that in every act of *poiesis* – making, creatively, some form that resolves given tensions between message and medium, giver and recipient, moral law and artistic excellence – you are participating in the Holy Spirit's renewal of the face of the earth. As culture-builders, we are all artists to some degree, bringing words of truth in communicable forms to the cultures we inhabit – family, church community, arts patronage, philanthropy, media, farming, business organization, etc.... Each of these areas has its own internal rules, laws, or constraints, by which the excellence of our forms will be judged. The artist is free, but works best when he works "in willing submission to the limitations of [his] own medium."[123]

**Art is a Form of Unity**

If we would communicate Christ through new artistic, verbal, and cultural forms, we must be in unity with His Church and able to place ourselves into unity with others. The Catholic artist does not live for himself, or in an exalted state above his fellow man, but in community and solidarity with others. Pope Benedict XVI, in *A New Song for the Lord*, warns against a vision of the artist that is contrary to Christian faith:

> ...aestheticism which excludes every function of art as service, that is which can only regard art

---

[122] St. Pope John Paul II, *Letter to Artists*, pg. 15
[123] Dorothy Sayers, *Mind of the Maker*, Chapter IV

> as having its own purpose and its own standard, is incompatible with the directives of the Bible. …to elevate the human person to the level of a pure creator…leads the human person into untruth, into contradiction with his or her own nature; …disintegration of what is creative. … the anthropological problem of the modern age… In idealistic philosophy the human spirit is no longer primarily receptive – it does not receive, but is only productive. …The human being comes from a meaningless factuality and is thrown into a meaningless freedom. The person thus becomes a pure creator; at the same time his or her creativity becomes a mere whim and, precisely for this reason, empty. According to Christian faith, however, it belongs to the essence of human beings that they come from God's 'art,' that they themselves are a part of God's art and as perceivers can think and view God's creative ideas with him and translate them into the visible and the audible. …to serve is not foreign to art; only by serving the Most High does it exist at all. …It is precisely the test of true creativity that the artist steps out of the esoteric circle and knows how to form his or her intuition in such a way that the others – the many – may perceive what the artist has perceived.[124]

Distortion in our understanding of the role of the artist in society makes it difficult for Catholic artists to imagine what forms a less-individualistic practice of art might take. Patrons of the arts and art educators, likewise, need help seeing clearly what it means for an artist to be offered to the world by God through the Body of Christ, His Church. The

---

[124] Pope Benedict XVI, *A New Song for the Lord*, pg. 133

person-centered communication model reminds the artist to turn 'back' toward his own personal integrity and 'forward,' toward the good of persons receiving his gifts. The Church-centered communication model reminds him to find both strength for extension into the culture and companionship in the adventure of collaborative creativity from the core strength of life in Christian community. In her writings about the spirituality of unity and its application to the arts, Focolare foundress Chiara Lubich said "Beauty found a place in our Movement because the word our charism began to speak to the world was one alone: unity. And unity means the highest harmony."[125]

**Art is Participation in Love**

The artist, like the teacher, like Christ, must condescend in love toward those to whom he gives his forms. Though he may not ever see the recipient of his gifts, or know him personally, he needs love to help him bridge the enormous gap that may exist between what he wants to convey and the recipient's capacity to receive it through form. The mind of the artist participates, in a small way, in the Trinitarian dimensions of all created form. Dorothy Sayers suggests that works of art rise from the artist's Idea, Energy, and Power to become structures that reveal correspondence between these aspects of 'artist' and the Father, Son, and Spirit of the Trinity.

> No incarnate Idea is altogether devoid of Power; if the Idea is feeble, the Energy dispersed, and the Power dim, the indwelling spirit will be dim,

---

[125] Chiara Lubich, *Essential Writings*, "The Charism of Unity and the Arts," pg. 310

dispersed and feeble.[126] ...The Power – the Spirit – is thus a social power, working to bring all minds into its own unity, sometimes by similarity and at other times by contrast.[127] ...the creator's love for his work is not a greedy possessiveness; he never desires to subdue his work to himself but always to subdue himself to his work. The more genuinely creative he is, the more he will want his work to develop in accordance with its own nature, and to stand independent of himself.[128] ... The imperfections of the artist may be conveniently classified as imperfections in his trinity.[129]

Failure in the 'Father' dimension is weakness in the clear idea of what we want to communicate. The figure has, perhaps, not quite risen from the ground of imagination clearly enough to be formed by the artist. Articulation, definition, and accuracy in correspondence to reality will sharpen the Idea. Failure in the 'Son' dimension is failure in the Energy, or struggle and work of taking the Idea into realization through form. Lack of patience, lack of skill with the materials, lack of effective effort and persistence, lack of discipline, and lack of submission to the Idea all lead to failure in the form. Failure in the 'Spirit' is failure to brood over and love the form, failure to affirm and release it as a free gift from God, failure to invite Love to resolve tension creatively, failure to work in unity with collaborators and those to whom the work will be given. Failures in the 'Spirit' compromise the Power of the form

---

[126] Dorothy Sayers, *The Mind of the Maker*, pg. 113
[127] Dorothy Sayers, *The Mind of the Maker*, pg. 121
[128] Dorothy Sayers, *The Mind of the Maker*, pg. 130
[129] Dorothy Sayers, *The Mind of the Maker*, pg. 149

to carry forth meaning and to have an impact as it moves away from the speaker, artist, founder, author, or builder.[130]

**Art Informs Evangelization**

Art forms, then, are 'arguments' that transcend the personal space-time of conversation, presence, dialogue, and the plane of contention. Of all forms of communication, they may involve the communicator most fully, but leave the least stamp of his presence in the work. Like the Creator, who so fully allows each form its own being, the artist is most veiled in his highest works. No wonder he seems to be something of a mythical god, reaching far beyond us into unknown territory to bring us sparks of divine fire that kindle answering flames in our hearts and hearths. Ultimately, communication of Christ *is* this *poiesis*, this making of ways, paths, bridges, forms, and persons by those who have stepped with Him into the eternal present.

Holly Ordway, closing her book, *Apologetics and the Christian Imagination*, describes imaginative apologetics as cooperation with a living Faith.

> ...the Faith can never be reduced to a single argument, or a single image, because it is a living thing. When we invite people to enter into the Church, we are inviting them to come home and, in so doing, also to explore a glorious new country, where there is always more to discover. We are inviting them to be made truly whole, as unique individuals, and also to discover the joyous fellowship of the communion of the saints, living

---

[130] See Chapter 11 - Possibilities of Form for more about Sayers' ideas on the artist's and the form's Trinitarian structure.

and dead. This is the vision we must try, as best we can, to share: that the universe is profoundly meaningful, that all things are interconnected in and through Christ, and that to be a Christian is to be fully alive, now and eternally. God is the ultimate Artist, and Author, and Composer: in his work, all creation sings, and each of us is called to join in the cosmic harmony.[131]

Middlework – the work of communicating Christ, reweaving the social fabric, participating in the movement of Love – is also a work of translation. Like the mythical hero, Prometheus, who returns with the fire of the gods, each Christian is the hero of the Real Myth, returning from the dead with the resurrected Christ, bringing the fire of the Spirit, and showing his fellow man the way into the Promised Land where the Father waits to meet him face to face. Middlework is the art of way-finding – moving into the gap of the missing middle to find a way where there is no way across the abyss or through the obstacle that looms between persons, or between persons and God. By stepping into Eternity, by identifying with Christ instead of a job, a mirror image, a rock star, or a superman, we have stepped out of the boundary of space-time into a territory that is far off from many persons' experience of reality – not just 'out of the cave,' but literally 'out of this world,' these structures, this present darkness, this moment.

The Reality you serve and the reality those who are 'of the world' live are incommensurable – so disproportionate that there is no 'way' between them. In the Golden Mean, we have the idea of a pivotal term that can link two such

---

[131] Holly Ordway, *Apologetics and the Christian Imagination*, pg. 177

things.[132] It stands in such relation to both other elements that they are brought into proportion, or relationship, through its presence. Because the Trinity was full of love, Christ became that term. Because He returned to the Father, the Spirit became that term. Because Mary accepted her role as mother of the Church, she stands in that golden relation to us. Because the Church is made Bride by supernatural power, she stands in the gap between the Kingdom and the world, as a mediating structure. Because you are enfolded into this enormous story as a chiastic center of its sweeping movement, you too serve as the Way – a lone rung on Wisdom's ladder of proportions – when you communicate Christ.

As an icon of the living God, your presence in the world is an interface to Him – a living instance of His presence. You are both 'ataphatic' (as an ataphatic icon is an image of the Trinity or one of the Persons of God and as you bear the image of God) and 'cataphatic' (as a cataphatic icon focuses the viewer's gaze through a saint who veils-and-thus-reveals the glory of God, and as Jesus is realized in and through each particular member of His Body). Your being testifies to your Creator, the One-in-Whom-All, and your works, when they carry the spark of living fire, testify

---

[132] From Vance G. Morgan, *Weaving the World: Weil on Science, Mathematics, and Love*, Notre Dame Press, 2005, pg. 151: "….the Greek search for mean proportional was prophetic of the greatest mean proportional of all, the Christ. …Weil wishes us to consider the incommensurability of many numbers with each other as a picture of the incommensurability between God and humanity. …finding mean proportional between incommensurables required thinking outside normal parameters, required an invasion from 'outside.' Precisely the same sort of activity outside normal limits is required to mediate between God and humanity."

that in every diverse form His glory may be found (in each, the All).[133]

This power to turn both upward and downward, God-ward and man-ward, inward and outward, to be both a "bi-polar extremist"[134] and an extreme gravitational center, and to be at once 'with' all that is not against Christ and 'against' all that is not for Him reveals you – the human person – to be a creative form that resolves paradoxical tension. This is not 'being two-faced,' but being "all things to all men," which Love's movement through your freedom makes possible.[135]

---

[133] See "The Four Types of Icon" by Vladislav Andrejev; Others use 'apophatic' and 'kataphatic,' but I have retained Andrejev's spelling as his article first informed me on this topic.

[134] Bishop Robert Barron: "…the chief problem we face in the Church is not lack of loyalty to Rome, not insufficient concern for the poor, not ignorance of women's concerns, not liturgical abuse, not theological imprecision, not resurgent triumphalism… is a lack of imagination, the inability to hold opposites in tension, the failure to be, boldly and unapologetically, bi-polar extremists."

[135] 1 Corinthians 9:22: "I have become all things to all men, that I might by all means save some."

Chapter 9

# Renewing the Culture

Scripture tells us that Christ is in our midst – in the 'space' between us. (Physical space is a metaphor for this space-between-us that participates in a dimension beyond the material-temporal world.) If we think of His kingdom coming as Christ *being realized in* – emerging into – our midst, then the concept of this space becomes quite interesting. It cannot be an empty void if it is full of the expectancy of His presence. The substantial hope of His coming supports and holds open the possibility of fullness there. The tension of two or more persons, joined together, creates a chamber where His word may open and resound. The faith of two or more in His Presence makes *of their unity* a space full of promise. The unity you establish with another person by loving intention (an *act* in itself) is form.

From the scale of a single person, up through the layers of his expanding circles of affiliation – family, friendship, local community, global solidarity, universal Church – Christ is realized in much the same way. We *are* forms; we generate, create and exchange forms; we take in and participate in forms through which He comes. Culture is the result of our 'form-building,' the aggregate of our Self-communication and communication of Christ, and the sphere of our relations. We rightly hope to watch that space for the full realization of Christ. To speak of bridging between sacred and secular culture is to miss the import of the Catholic, sacramental perspective. The holy is already here, as all Creation, all form declares the glory of God. Wherever we are when we communicate Christ becomes holy ground.

Culture is the turbulent, transitional, messy space between us, where we "work out our salvation with fear and trembling," experience glimpses of the emerging kingdom, encounter the needs and perspectives of neighbors, and are pierced by the light of glory shining out from surprising places. Culture – our conversations, religion and ethics, education and formation, use of material resources and stewardship of the environment, transactions and institutions, and our works of art – is an exciting and terrifying arena. There, the fruits of our relationships with our fellow man are expressed, and there is the ground that nourishes those relationships. Culture is both the 'content' and 'context' of the becoming of Man.[136]

For Christians, Christ-in-His-Church is the context-within-which we remain (more enormous than the world, or culture) and we are vessels within which He remains (deeply embedded within and generative of culture). Our forms (church buildings, events, rituals) invite Others into the Presence, and our forms (songs, sculptures, invitations) light the way in, articulate the path, and fill the atmosphere with hope.

### What is Man, That We Should Be Mindful of Him?

Man – see him all around you: broken and bent, poisoned by lies, deformed, powerless, enslaved, disintegrated,

---

[136] Thoughts from this paragraph forward to the end of Chapter 9 are replicated, to some extent, in my unpublished mss *Souls at Play*.

barren, lonely, ignorant, blind. Yet the emptiness within him is yearning toward the Faith that would fill him, the Hope that would lead him, the Love that would complete him. Even in his debased state, he is brave, beautiful, talented, generous, capable, amazing. Who could bear the glory of a man fully formed, virtuous, free? He could not. No man bears the weight of his own being, but lives and moves within the Being who holds that fullness for him. Like a garment he must grow big enough to wear, his destiny awaits. He cannot inhabit the vast space of his own being, yet to become able, he must continually try. And we must help him.

But who can bear the impossible paradox of man's lowness and his highness? We cannot. We, who struggle alongside him toward our own destinies have but little capacity for such tension. His lowness frightens and disgusts us, and his highness is veiled in mystery. We cannot penetrate, or comprehend, or bear, or raise our fellow man. We cannot reconcile him to himself. But there is One who can, who stands in the gap between the real and the ideal, between actuality and destiny, between emptiness and fulfillment, between man and the God he has rejected.

Christ is the creative resolution of the high-tension paradox that is man. He is the creative response, the new beginning, the bridge, the re-strung warp for the reweaving of the garment, the clear organizing principle, the law, the interior support for man's standing up, and for his freedom of movement toward his destiny. So, we, who are the Body of Christ, must help to re-place Christ at the center of man.

If only fallen man would take Him in, give Him shelter, embrace Him, hear Him, do Him justice, taste and see that He is good. But man has very little capacity to do so.

How far must He go, how small must He be, how must He be veiled to be given entrance to flattened, reduced, organization man? And, if there is no capacity left in man – even for a crumb, a word – what then? What rich, supportive, nourishing context will He build around a man to sustain him while that primal urge to be himself awakens; while the impress of God's image upon him becomes a capacity for life, for crumbs, for Christ?

We *know* how far Love would go, how small the form He would take, and how distressing the disguises He would wear to win a man. We *know* a Body broken into crumbs, Truth reduced into words, a perfect Womb woven to mediate wisdom and grace to a man in his becoming, a vessel emptied of all but love. We *know*, but we may not yet emulate such love. When that Love fills us, is fully realized in us, we, too, will speak words of Truth, create small forms filled with sustenance, lay our lives down as paths, and communicate Christ to man.

But how to love man, such as he is? Chiara Lubich, speaking of the theology of unity, recognizes that 'unity in the bond of love' with our fellow man is made possible only by identification with Christ, on the Cross, forsaken. This love has taken such pity on man as to set aside all but love to make unity with man possible. The moment of His forsakenness speaks to our hearts of the common bond we have with every other man: our utter dependence on the life of Christ, given for us in Love. If we can first extend ourselves in this unity with him, we can grow in love by deepening our understanding of the person we encounter. We love as we *know*. So we must know, must ask, must interest ourselves in the question, "Who is Man?"

Who is man that Christ would die for him? Who is man that God would form him, raise him, build him up, give him freedom, fill him with His own image? Who is man that God would place Creation under his dominion? Who is man that God would give him a place in His household, and a role in the distribution of His wealth? Who is man that God would allow him to re-present immaterial Reality, untouchable purity, incomprehensible mystery? These questions about man are answered – rightly, or wrongly – in the five primary 'disciplines' of, or components of culture.

**Disciplines of Culture**

Within the cultural spheres of Religion, Education, Creation, Economics, and Art are accumulations of man's responses, in a sense, to these essential questions about himself. Those responses then in-form our children, our friends, and the aliens in our midst, for good or ill. Culture may be the context of our struggle to become who we truly are, but it is not the initial context of our being, or the context of our destinies. The Person of God, Himself, and the 'new heavens and new earth' where we will inhabit our eternal 'mansions' hold those further dimensions open for us. St. Pope John Paul has said that what the world desperately needs is a 'recapitulation of man.' Our approach to culture-building can help in this recapitulation, by which man may be reflected back to himself *as* himself from within the eyes of Love, where the whole truth is held for him as in a living mirror.

We are, in a sense, educating man, proposing new truths to him about himself. Our forms – our communication of Christ – may move through the horizontal, cultural dimension to relight the Eternal flame in our fellow man. Fr. Giussani speaks of this fire we hope to light:

> Communication that has become appealing and evocative is the beginning of the cultural phenomenon; it is the fire that ignites it. This happens when the student – or anyone else for that matter – meets an adult whose very presence is a proposal for an explanation, for an explanatory hypothesis of life. ...There are two features to this cultural rebirth: (a) This phenomenon awakens in the student an interest in everything. If he has run into an all-encompassing proposal, then everything becomes familiar to him...(b) A cultural phenomenon will become a fire and spread only if it springs from a deep-seated certainty. This certainty I speak of is Christ's coming.... ...the process of humanizing the world, something made possible by the cultural phenomenon, coincides with Christianizing the world. Christ makes us participants in his work.[137]

You can think of each sphere of culture as a 'discipline'. The word 'discipline' indicates a mixture of theory and practice, makes allusion to the need for inter-disciplinary thought, and implies that the student must first be a disciple, or follower. Following Christ, the Christian who would evangelize the culture must discipline himself to the practice of community – the living of life with and for others in actuality and practice. Not only must he follow Christ, but must follow the indications manifest in the Church, expressed as supernaturally protected treasures of lucid teaching and historical continuity, which articulate

---

[137] Luigi Giussani, *The Risk of Education*, Chapter 3

a reliable path through time for the cultural project of the emerging Kingdom of God.

Here, within this Catholic context, we first situate ourselves in docile continuity with the Church, her Pope, her Magisterium, her Tradition, and her authority – the only solid place from which to begin any conversation about cultural renewal. We orient ourselves within the living stream of Catholic theological guidelines for cultural renewal and thus grow in clarity about our role as Christ's living realization and response to the realities that we encounter. Then we can place ourselves 'in conversation with' some of the responses being made in the world around us. We need practice in this sort of engagement with ideas, though there is no necessity that we engage with every possible alternative to Catholic thought. The core strength of Catholic culture, experienced within Catholic community, should allow for some degree of extension into fruitful dialogue with others.

The nature of any study of culture is intensely inter-disciplinary. There is, in reality, no way to consider any one of the areas without overstepping into others. In fact, you may truly say that *each* of the five disciplines is *in* all the others. The many areas of culture that do not seem to be given place – such as politics, law, science, medicine, and the interior life of spirituality and prayer – are assumed to be implied in the five major disciplines. There are endless possibilities for fruitful cross-pollination of elements, and for new insights to develop from juxtaposing the disciplines in various combinations. It's exciting and delightful! I hope to provide a first-pathway through a territory that merits much more exploration.

**Religion is Central**

The sphere of Religion must – if the human person is to be re-placed at the center of culture – be a central discipline, or fountain pouring out into each of the other spheres. It is unique in that it emerges from the deep religious sense in man – a sense that precedes and then informs all his other culture building.[138] It can also be seen as the overarching context for all other cultural development, since man's movement toward his destiny and yearning toward the Divine mind is the context for his relationships, work, and way-finding – all of which result in the forms that fill the cultural spheres. To imagine Religion as, simply, another sphere of culture, self-expression, man-initiated form, or individualistic imaginal structure is to do the human person a grave disservice.

The playing field, stage, or battleground of culture (complex and interesting as it is) is a relatively 'flat' terrain of temporal, spatial endeavor – without scope enough for man in his wholeness. Yet Christ has deigned to enter here, and we will do well to follow Him. Cultural forms – systems of ethics and law, human institutions and inventions, literature, art, and all the rest – that give 'flat' answers to the questions we've posed are, likewise, insufficient to supply man's wholeness, or his full realization.

Catholics are called to fill culture with Christ, with His love for man, with His words that articulate the path back to correspondence with reality and Holy Wisdom. We must know man for the wonder he is, know Christ for the God He is, and lay down all that we are, all that we have, to mediate between them. Our words, our oil paints and watercolors,

---

[138] See: Luigi Giussani, *The Religious Sense*

our clubs and families and businesses, our needs and yearnings, struggles, concerns, interests, passions – whatever the materials we offer – can be used to convey light, communicate Christ, hold open space for the coming of the Kingdom by God, who weaves together all things for good.

We need to take the risk of asking these essential questions, considering the answers our Church – ever concerned with the being, becoming, and destiny of man and his full realization in Christ – proposes. We must each discover man's yearnings, man's emptiness, man's greatness, man's glory in ourselves and verify that Christ truly *is* the Way, the Truth and the Light that lead to our own destinies; *is* the Presence in us who makes glorious freedom possible; *is* the turning point of all history whose Resurrection power continues to emerge in and through the unities and forms we create.

In some approaches to culture, religion is understood as one manifestation of culture, or as a man-made institution. It is common to see culture understood as many distinct and autonomous spheres of human activity with no common reference point. Another misunderstanding of culture is to think of it as reduced to the power struggle between opposing groups. We cannot accept these reductions of a fully human idea of culture without undermining our own contributions to culture. The religious sense which results from contact with the Reality of a Creator grounds every other cultural expression in the original Presence of Christ. To remove the human person as the central focus of culture is to remove that Presence. Granted that, absent the full-dimensionality of man, vacuums will result and be exploited by those with a will to power, we cannot let 'what power would do' become the limit for 'what Love would do'! Our creativity, responsiveness, generativity, and joy will be oppressed and dampened if we focus on the ever-more-confused culture and cultural analysis provided by the blind for the blind.

**A Verbal Scaffolding Supports Our Work**

The role of words, of verbal structures, of articulation has already been stressed, but I cannot overemphasize the need for rebuilding, strengthening, and redeeming words in our day. Much of the cultural support for the disintegration of man involves the deconstruction of verbal structures such as literature and law, the emptying of meaning from words, or the subtle reshaping of word meanings to accommodate various agendas and power-plays. (The convenient way that pregnancy is now said to begin with 'implantation,' rather than with 'conception' is a case in point.) Words are the indispensable means by which Truth takes its throne in the context of conversation, dialogue, apologetics, argument, and art. When words are not the media used directly in the making of art, they are still foundational as the *logos*, or logic from which works of art may communicate Christ.

For our creative and responsive acts of cultural renewal to be linked to supernatural grace adequately, and to express Christ fully and truthfully, we first consciously orient ourselves in docility to the authority of Christ as expressed by means of His Church. The theological work that continuously articulates the 'narrow way' of Christ through the errors and distortions of truth surrounding us is largely invisible to us, yet undergirds our action with a matrix of support for our freedom and creativity.

In this, the work of the best minds, or thought leaders of the Church corresponds to the invisible matrix of Holy Wisdom which preceded the created order and continues to undergird its coherent development over time. We owe a debt to those who have engaged in theological argument, for their work emerges as a framework, or lens through which we can orient our own response to the culture in living continuity with the teachings of Christ. Without such guidance, we are in danger of being influenced, instead, by thought leaders in secular culture whose work, likewise invisible and powerfully pervasive, shapes the culture of death, despair and unbelief.

None of us debates Truth in an original way, but we all first trust others on reasonable grounds and then view reality through the lens formed within us on the basis of that trust. It is, obviously, critically important to trust trustworthy thought leaders in order to benefit from their correction of our own errors and inadequacies. To paraphrase G.K. Chesterton, we need a Church that is right not only where we are right, but one that is right where we are wrong. If one of us reveals a mistaken understanding, we can be gently corrected by loving community on the basis of the clear teaching of the Church. God will shake what can be shaken, and continually reforms the structural flaws thus exposed.

Not only are we supported by an infrastructure of creed, dogma, intellectual tradition and Magisterial teaching, we are embraced by the very Mother of Mother Church, whose influence on culture is enormous. Carrie Gress, in *The Marian Option*, describes Mary's role in preparing the world for Jesus:

In the Litany of Our Lady of Sorrows, her more militant side shines through. In it, she is called Shield of the oppressed, Conqueror of the incredulous, Protectress of those who fight, Haven of the shipwrecked, Calmer of tempests, Retreat of those who groan, Terror of the treacherous, and Standard-bearer of the Martyrs...In the military battles where she is invoked, the scale is tipped in surprising ways for her warriors.[139]

Mary's influence...doesn't stop at routing enemies; it extends into transforming the landscape. She fortifies the community and country through the workings of culture. ...when Marian devotion flourishes, so too does culture. Mary as our mother brings order to those places where she is invoked and honored.[140]

Through such men as St. Bernard, St. Albert, and St. Thomas, Mary has also been known as the Destroyer of Heresies. ...How does she destroy heresies? ...She does it...by inspiring zeal.[141]

**What Is Culture Anyway?**

The word 'culture' means different things to various people and in various settings. You may have noticed some of these meanings:

- Behaviors and beliefs of a particular social or ethnic group

---

[139] Carrie Gress, *The Marian Option*, Pg. 20,21
[140] Carrie Gress, *The Marian Option*, Pg. 26
[141] Carrie Gress, *The Marian Option*, Pg. 34

- All the behaviors and artifacts of ways of life in a group of human beings

- Ways of life transmitted from one generation to another

- To inhabit, care for, or till the soil of a place

- The cultivation of soul, or mind

- Aesthetic excellence

- Patterns of human knowledge, belief and behavior

- Shared attitudes, morals, values and customs

Some commonalities among these definitions are that culture involves human persons and their relationships, beliefs, and values. It has to do with the forms by which they express themselves and teach those beliefs and values within human relationships. Culture extends from individuals to build and sustain bonds of community, and time. Culture then becomes a context that influences action, affects our shared lives, and helps to multiply the 'seeds of value' embodied in it.

When Catholics use the word, it takes on a richness and depth that is very attractive. Far from being opposed to, or at war with culture, Catholics have a positive, multi-dimensional understanding that arises from an awareness of and insight into the human person. Examples of specifically Catholic usage of the word are found in the Catechism, two encyclicals, and the final document of the Vatican's Pontifical Council for Culture.

> To promote the participation of the greatest number in the life of a society, the creation of voluntary

associations and institutions must be encouraged "on both national and international levels, which relate to economic and social goals, to cultural and recreational activities, to sport, to various professions, and to political affairs."[142]

The experience of past ages, the progress of the sciences, and the treasures hidden in the various forms of human culture, by all of which the nature of man himself is more clearly revealed and new roads to truth are opened, these profit the Church, too. For, from the beginning of her history she has learned to express the message of Christ with the help of the ideas and terminology of various philosophers, and has tried to clarify it with their wisdom, too.[143]

To promote such exchange, especially in our days, the Church requires the special help of those who live in the world, are versed in different institutions and specialties, and grasp their innermost significance in the eyes of both believers and unbelievers. With the help of the Holy Spirit, it is the task of the entire People of God, especially pastors and theologians, to hear, distinguish and interpret the many voices of our age, and to judge them in the light of the divine word, so that revealed truth can always be more deeply penetrated, better

---

[142] *Catechism of the Catholic Church: Modifications from the Editio Typica.*, Second ed. Vatican: Libreria Editrice Vaticana, 1997. Paragraph 1882, citing John XXII, *Mater et Magistra* 60. See also the whole of Chapter Two, "The Human Community," pg.459-472
[143] St. Pope John Paul II, *Gaudium et spes*, 22

understood and set forth to greater advantage. Since the Church has a visible and social structure as a sign of her unity in Christ, she can and ought to be enriched by the development of human social life, not that there is any lack in the constitution given her by Christ, but that she can understand it more penetratingly, express it better, and adjust it more successfully to our times.[144]

Culture only exists through man, by man and for man. It is the whole of human activity, human intelligence and emotions, the human quest for meaning, human customs and ethics. Culture is so natural to man that human nature can only be revealed through culture. In a pastoral approach to culture, what is at stake is for human beings to be restored in fullness to having been created "in the image and likeness of God" (*Gen* 1:26), tearing them away from the anthropocentric temptation of considering themselves independent from the Creator. Therefore, and this observation is crucial to a pastoral approach to culture, "it must certainly be admitted that man always exists in a particular culture, but it must also be admitted that man is not exhaustively defined by that same culture. Moreover, the very progress of cultures demonstrates that there is something in man which transcends those cultures. This 'something' is precisely human nature: this nature is itself the measure of culture and the condition of ensuring that man does not become prisoner of any of his

---

[144] St. Pope John Paul II, *Gaudium et spes*, 44

> cultures, but asserts his personal dignity by living in accordance with the profound truth of his being"[145]
>
> In a perspective of Gospel preparation, the primary objective of the pastoral approach to culture, is to inject the life-blood of the Gospel into cultures to renew from within and transform in the light of the Revelation the visions of men and society that shape cultures, the concepts of men and women, of the family and of education, of school and of university, of freedom and of truth, of labour and of leisure, of the economy and of society, of the sciences and of the arts.[146]

A Catholic, transcendent sense of culture rooted in the truth about the human person and his unity with all men under their common Creator not only considers the common interests and needs of all persons, nations and cultural sub-groups, but also unifies all the spheres in which the self-development of individuals generates cultural forms and norms. A human-centered approach to culture links man's activities in the arts, at home, in his economic decisions and institutions to his own eternal destiny.

Bishop Robert Barron has suggested that, in our engagement with culture, we can transcend some of the divisive polarizations among persons by being 'bi-polar extremists' – going beyond the reductions of every extremist position to demonstrate the possibility of transcendence in a Catholic 'position' above the plane of tension. Another way of phrasing that might be to say that

---

[145] *Veritatis Splendor*, 53, cited in *Towards a Pastoral Approach*, by Pontifical Council for Culture, Vatican, June 9, 1999, 25
[146]

Catholic 'way' is an 'extreme centrism' – rising above polarized positions to resolve that tension in a truly 'new thing.' A response-in-form can invite our fellow man to freedom in Christ.

**Mary Cultivates Christians**

The project 'renew the culture' is far beyond the scope of this book, and yet is the real possibility indicated by the renewal of the human person as he communicates Christ. The project 'communicate Christ' is made up of individual-scale projects through which His being emerges like a photo develops pixel-by-pixel into higher resolution. The tiny, fractal repetition of the project 'be free' (made possible for each of us by the indwelling Trinity) should expand to fill the cultural dimension with truly new forms that radiate the invitation to, indicate the path toward, lift up the lived example of, form that resonates with human freedom. The Blessed Mother is intimately involved with the growth and development of her Son in His Church, and His realization into the world through us.

**Culture Building is Non-Linear**

While we are primarily interested in creating a strong 'Catholic culture,' we cannot afford to focus exclusively on the excellent goal of robust expression of Catholicity in rituals, prayer, events, traditions, conversations, relationships and works of art. A 'linear' approach waits until some first thing is perfect before work begins on a second, but culture building is work on many trajectories at once. If we turn outward only when our Catholic culture is 'strong enough,' the world will be waiting a long time! Obviously, we can't extend into cultural engagement without the risk of being thrown off balance and weakening our primary, Sacramental, ecclesial and familial being. Yet, if we don't extend and take risks at all, we will not develop in a fully rounded, or three-dimensional way. The extension that reveals core weakness is a positive element in this whole-person growth. The demands made for collaborative response by the Body of Christ to the needs of those perishing in the world strengthen the Church.

Our strength to reach into the culture beyond the Church is grounded in the richness of our 'Catholic culture' at the core of life in the society of others. That culture is not to become a hidey-hole protecting us from engagement with the world, but a mediating structure enabling us to extend further out. Catholic culture, if it closes in on itself, will implode and wither in power to communicate Christ. "…cultures require a certain type of regeneration in order to sustain themselves; the culture will fall to pieces without new lifeblood. This lifeblood comes…by having one generation raise the next generation into spiritual adulthood. Few parents think of the essential reality of bringing their children to spiritual adulthood. …spiritual immaturity is something Our Mother eradicates. Even the children to whom she has appeared, though tender of age, showed incredible signs of spiritual maturity."[147]

Gress goes on to cite Archbishop Fulton Sheen:

> Culture derives from woman – for had she not taught her children to talk, the great spiritual values of the world would not have passed from generation to generation. After nourishing the substance of the body to which she gave birth, she then nourishes the

---

[147] Carrie Gress, *The Marian Option*, pg. 179

> child with the substance of her mind. As guardian of the values of the spirit, as protectress of the morality of the young, she preserves culture, which deals with purposes and ends, while man upholds civilization, which deals only with means.[148]

Mary, Mother Church, Woman and 'with' strength are needed to recover culture's integrity as a 'womb' within which free persons may be formed. Our Blessed Mother is actively regenerating our small forms of community, through which we "grow up in all things unto Christ."[149]

We've looked at the way love transforms work into art, since message-with-love form-making is fundamental to our becoming, our contribution to culture, and our communication of Christ. Charity-in-Truth (truth as a vessel for love, or a seed of supportive infrastructure) is the organizing principle for the Church's response to reality. The opening principle for expansive movement of the new *logos* into the spheres of Art, Creation, Economics and Education is Truth-in-Love (seeds of truth draped in the fruit of the Spirit, or truth spoken in a charity which enables the listener to receive it). In the next chapter, we'll dip into those vast cultural spheres for a taste of all the good that might be done by following our inclinations to communicate Christ wherever our interests take us.

As we go forward, may we be deeply influenced by, and docile to our Blessed Mother.

> Let us let ourselves be led, then; let us *peaceful, peaceful*; let us not attempt to do *more* than that which she wills or *more quickly*. Let us let ourselves

---

[148] Carrie Gress, *The Marian Option*, pg. 183,184
[149] Ephesians 4:15: "...speaking the truth in love, we are to grow up in every way into him who is the head, into Christ."

be carried by her; she will think of everything and take care of all our needs, of the soul and of the body. Let us give every difficulty, every sorrow to her, and have confidence that she will take care of it better than we could. *Peace*, then, peace, much *peace* in an unlimited confidence in her.[150]

---

[150] St. Maximilian Kolbe, cited in Carrie Gress, *The Marian Option*, pg. 187

# Chapter 10

# In Conversation with Culture

As our desire to communicate Christ takes us further and further from more homogenous 'we's to increasingly heterogenous 'they's, the common ground shrinks and we encounter more errors. Preparation for error begins in education and in the intellectual life of reading, writing, and conversation. Contrasting, or even conflicting positions have a place in our intellectual development. Paul Griffiths, in *Intellectual Appetite*, says "Carefully descriptive juxtaposition of opposed or otherwise contrasting views, coupled with the making and offering of precise and perspicuous distinctions, is almost always more productive than argument, whether aimed at refutation of an opposed position or defence of one's own."[151] A. G. Sertillanges, in *The Intellectual Life*, agrees:

> An essential condition for profiting by our reading…is to tend always to reconcile our authors instead of setting one against another. …the fruitful research is to look for points of contact. … Especially in regard of very great minds it is a sort of profanation to adopt a fault-finding attitude. Let us regret their errors, but without violent condemnation; let us build bridges, not ditches between their doctrines. …To address oneself to this work of reconstituting the integral truth out of

---

[151] Paul Griffiths, *Intellectual Appetite*, pg. 4

its misinterpretations is far more fruitful than to be perpetually criticizing.[152]

The revolutionary way to move people from one position to another is to cause a radical break in the continuum connecting them. "These two things are antithetical. If you would have the x, y, z (goods) offered by position B you must break utterly with position A," or "The negatives clearly apparent in position A necessitate a break with it, and a move to position B." Destabilized by the difficulty of holding to both A and B, or to the good in both, those persuaded to break with A will swing (probably briefly) to B, then find a less extreme, more tenable position A1 that is a bit nearer to B. Repetition of this 'radical break' methodology is meant to lead ever closer to B by steps A1, A2, A3, etc… We might call this an 'omnivocal'[153] approach in which, because we don't believe there is a way of listening to a higher Voice, we force and manipulate one controlling idea to dominate the noise of all ideas at war.

A revolutionist sets up a false dualism between two positions in order to push thought toward his organizing principle, or position. Because this approach is associated with 'Marxist dialectics,' the whole concept of arguing our way to truth is sometimes rejected as 'relativism'. If truth is to be relative to your age, your culture, your feelings, then there is no secure and stable place to stand, and

---

[152] A. G. Sertillanges, *The Intellectual Life*, pg. 164

[153] Or, as in Mattias Desmet's *The Psychology of Totalitarianism*, 'monosemy,' as opposed to the natural 'polysemy' of human language which allows for layers of meaning to attend words. Fear reduces our capacity to receive the richness of nuance, metaphor and contextual support for meaning, hence those who would dominate us use fear to destroy the middle ground of civic conversation.

personhood will be undermined. But, to place ideas into tension for the purpose of strengthening your grasp on truth by argument is the focus of 'dialectic,' as the word is used for the second stage of classical education. Learning to work with ideas in tension develops the capacity to respond to reality creatively and effectively. A completely univocal approach simply stands at A and rejects everything that is Not-A, in defense against any tension between ideas. The mind thus held rigid is unable to be affected by, or to be in correspondence with, reality.

An equivocal[154] approach that is not merely false compromise with error is illustrated by John Henry Newman's hypothetical Mr. Milman:

> Mr. Milman argues… "These things are in heathenism, therefore they are not Christian." We, on the contrary, prefer to say, "these things are in Christianity, therefore they are not heathen." That is, we prefer to say, and we think that Scripture bears us out in saying, that from the beginning the Moral Governor of the world has scattered the seeds of truth far and wide over its extent; that these have variously taken root, and grown up as in the wilderness, wild plants indeed but living; and hence that, as the inferior animals have tokens of an immaterial principle in them, yet have not souls, so the philosophies and religions of men have their life in certain true ideas, though they are not directly divine.[155]

---

[154] See William F. Lynch, Christ and Apollo for more on equivocality.
[155] Bl. J.H. Newman, "Milman's View of Christianity," 1871

Newman continues, "one special way in which Providence has imparted divine knowledge to us has been by enabling her [the Church] to draw and collect it together out of the world." Our practice with error in the home, in our reading and conversation, prepares us to resolve the tension we are bound to feel when something in a contrary position resonates with us as true, good, or beautiful. Likewise, we will see flaws in the thinking of those we revere and agree with in large part – a similar tension that tempts us to throw babies out with bathwater, or to relax in a comfortable, but extreme position.

If seeds of truth – *semina verbi* [156] – have indeed been scattered widely, Love's way is to encourage them wherever they are found, and to weed the garden without harming the seedlings. The more we are dealing with an actual person, the more 'with' strength we must wield, for his sake, in engagement with his ideas. The more our focus is on the ideas themselves, the more 'against' strength we can wield without violating the persons behind them. Love condescends to find a way to plant a seed, to build a bridge, to make a way where there is no way. As a person, you are a living mediating structure between Christ and those you encounter – not a fortress protecting Christ from the Other.

Those who attempt to force mental breakdown so that persons will clutch at paths and positions made of lies are

---

156    Francis Cardinal George: "The inculturation of the faith – the conversion of a society and culture brought about by preaching who Christ is in a language understandable to the people – begins with identifying semina verbi present in every culture and then moves to identify the demonic elements also present in any culture," in *The Difference God Makes*, Crossroad, 2009, pg. 127

violating both Truth and those persons. If we hold so rigidly to Truth that we dare make no path, refuse the possibility of learning from someone who is not perfectly orthodox, or pridefully imagine no error is possible in our own position, we violate, likewise, both the Truth (which has nothing to fear from conversation) and human beings.

Truth must comprehend error, and there is a place to stand to see all things more clearly – the narrow way of Christ-in-His-Church. But you are not necessarily the perfect knower, interpreter, or embodiment of Christ, and must yourself be comprehended, exposed to those on the 'other side' who can see lack in you that you cannot see in yourself. The more you hide from exposure, the more you resist correction that may come through people you have seen, in your pride, as 'wrong' and thus inferior. Perhaps the Other is invited to encounter with you because he needs to be shown a path to Truth. You may be invited to encounter with him because you need to be shown a lack of charity, logic, humility, or clarity in your communication of Truth which interferes with the communication of Christ.

**Tastes of Truth**

Because culture springs from "an interest in the perfection of the world,"[157] every sphere of culture involves us in some aspect of this perfecting – of Creation, of the world of exchange, of a work of art, or of a human person. The religious sense and religious worship at the center of all culture orders our cultural expressions to the goodness of man's *being*, and culture can be seen as the result of all our

---

[157] Hans Urs von Balthasar, *Convergences*, pg. 153

*doing*. That doing can be ordered toward, or away from, perfecting the world – your choice.

As you enter into the spheres of culture, you'll be becoming a mediating structure between the forms you encounter and the Church. You communicate Christ by connecting Him to the persons you encounter through books, conversations, cultural events, works of art, institutions and actions which place your ideas and values into forms. You communicate Christ by responding to whatever you encounter as a member of His Body, the Church – gifting to others the clarity and strength you've received through her resources, and returning to Her with the fruits of your listening. Communicating through forms is a two-way process. Your capacity to see through, to receive, to comprehend meaning held in forms is, ultimately, capacity for persons. Practice of the presence of persons has been stretching your capacity for them since you were born, and thus is expanding your capacity for Christ.

Practice of engagement with forms expands your power to communicate in forms and, so, to communicate Christ. The outward movement of the inner development is the response, the *poiesis*, the work that embodies, or incarnates, your message, your experience, your values, or your desires and so is the making of *you*. The interior stillness that is spaciousness, freedom, and trust allows for love to flow through you into forms as various as man's imagination.

First, rest in Christ (ideally, at perfect peace). Then, voice (ideally, with perfect love) Christ's response to whatever provokes you. Notice, evaluate, and learn from your imperfections and failure. Repeat. Fail over and over and over to communicate Christ, and He will both work in you to accomplish His purposes through you,[158] and perfect the work He has begun in you.[159] If you extend too far beyond your core strength, you'll fail, but not forward. If you never extend from your core, you'll fail, but not forward. Communication is a dynamic, two-way movement, not a static, safe position. You are refreshed by the Eucharist to go out and fail forward!

Practice in your 'we' circles, but also practice across a few 'they' lines as you grow. Move forward where your interests take you, and move back to collect, in yourself, the resources, skills, knowledge and other materials you'll need to build outward in these spheres of cultural engagement.

**The Sphere of Art**

Catholics should have a sacramental view of the world. The Sacraments entrusted to the Church are signs which actually convey the grace they represent. They demonstrate the potential of a form to be infused by, and thus to convey to some degree, real encounter with the thing being represented, and with the creator behind the form. To develop your capacity to receive and to make art forms you must learn to resolve tension creatively. The poet juxtaposes 'tree' and 'person' to explore one by the metaphor of the other; the painter resolves the tensions between figure and ground, light and shadow; the composer sets two themes at play 'against' each other, and resolves the tension in a third fugue theme. To receive well, you

---

[158] Philippians 2:13: "for it is God who works in you to will and to act in order to fulfill his good purpose."
[159] Philippians 1:6: "he who began a good work in you will perfect it"

need an interior spaciousness within which form may take its own shape and affect you. C. S. Lewis refers to this receptivity as 'surrender'.[160]

That surrender is in tension with your critical faculty, your emotional aversion to the material, and your tendency to place a label on and dismiss potentially uncomfortable encounters. Since there are similar tensions involved with the 'practice of persons,' you can say that expanding your receptive and creative capacities expands your capacity for persons, and thus for Christ. In fact, it may be that only your concern for an actual person (the artist, or someone who loves this work of art) will motivate you past those tensions into the territory of engagement with art forms that are jarring, ugly, awful, or confusing to you.

The practice of art in one medium improves your skill in another. Flannery O'Connor, for example, recommended drawing to writers to develop their eye for reality. Art, then, expands your 'correspondence to reality,' and, thus, your freedom. Work (receptive and creative) in art forms of every kind develops your 'metaphoric dimension'[161] or

---

[160] C.S. Lewis, in *An Experiment in Criticism*, pg. 19: "The first demand any work of art makes upon us is surrender."
[161] Charlotte Ostermann, *Souls at Play – Reflections on Creativity and Culture*, unpublished mss: "The practice of art develops what I have called the Metaphoric Dimension of personhood – the much-needed "ability to hold opposites in tension" that Fr. Barron finds lacking among 'beige' Catholics, the capacity for nuance, or what Cardinal George has called 'the analogical sense'. This dimension involves moving and being moved: active and passive participation in integrating, whole-making, form-generating movement. The person at the center of that movement expands in wholeness – from disintegrated dualism to three-dimensional integration, from flattened to spherical being, from communion to communication, and through community to Communion. God is, says Barron, "a back-and-forth of love". When we surrender to that loving movement, we become more fully who we truly are. As we grow in dimensionality, or realization, we become more and more able to take in and to communicate meaning, whether it is contained in words, art forms, or festive celebrations."

'analogic sense'[162]– helping you to think from one thing to another, to reweave a continuum between polarized extremes, to detect layers of meaning within prose and poetry, to gaze along a beam of light[163] or through a form to see what is veiled, to see negative space creatively, and to receive persons as works of art.

Unless Art is actively challenging and changing you, it is not communicating, moving, or becoming *you*. Please resist the temptation to agree – in theory – that art is good, valuable, or important, but never to practice engagement in the sphere of Art. If I seem to give the Sphere of Art short shrift here, it is because throughout this book, I have already pointed to art, or *poiesis* as the task of resolving tensions, making works of art, collaborating in the making of Self, and creating verbal generative structures in response to the realities we face. Your practice of Art is essential to the task of communicating Christ.

---

[162] Francis Cardinal George, *The Difference God Makes*, pg. 47: "....at the heart of the medieval Catholic theological worldview was a metaphysics of *participatio*. ...This analogical conception of being allowed the medieval to see God in creation and thus to appreciate the essential connectedness of all things to God and, through God, to one another....linked ...in the deepest ground of their existence....This vision began to break down under the influence of Duns Scotus's univocal conception of being (which turned God into a supreme instance of being, set over and against finite realities) and Nominalism (which radically individualized and hence separated God and creatures)."

[163] C.S. Lewis, in "Meditation in a Toolshed": "We must, on pain of idiocy, deny from the very outset the idea that looking at is, by its own nature, intrinsically truer or better than looking along. One must look both along and at everything."

**The Sphere of Creation**

The created world is a primary encounter with the beauty that may attract us into the work of art.[164] It provides lived experience with the dynamics of equilibrium and movement, the mystery of gender, chemical bonds, ecology, catalytic reactions, organic forms and systems, gravity, light and sound. These can, analogically, inform our social structures, physical health, technologies and literature. If man has been placed into the world to realize it fully, to return it to God fulfilled by his affirmation, understanding, stewardship, and analogical ascent to the matrix of Holy Wisdom, then Creation cannot be either a resource to exploit, or a god to worship.

Father Giussani taught that the 'I' is awakened by encounter with reality. Catholic, sacramental thought is united on this point: nature is not inert, but actively impacts those with eyes to see and ears to hear it. Many adults and children suffer these days from what Richard Louv, in *Last Child in the Woods,* calls "nature deficit disorder". Nature therapy is now used to counteract various mental, physical and emotional disorders. When the Church teaches that concern for creation is of the essence of human being, she is not parroting a modern fad, but recalling us to

---

[164] *The Via Pulchritudinus* (March 27, 2006 Plenary Assembly Concluding Document) III.1A: "…from the contemplation of the countryside at the setting of the sun, or snow-capped mountain summits under a starry sky, or fields covered with light-drenched flowers, or the varieties of plants and animals, there is born a palette of sentiments that invite us to read within (*intus-legere*), to pass from the visible to reach the invisible and give an answer to the question, "who is this Artisan with such powerful imagination at the origin of so much beauty and grandeur, such profusion of beings in the sky and on the earth?" At the same time, the contemplation of the beauties of creation causes an interior peace and sharpens the sense of harmony and the desire for a beautiful life."

ancient wisdom. If we feel punished, or restricted by the demands creation makes on us in its current state of deep neediness, we are missing the Church's message about our own profound need of nature's restoration, and of rightly-ordered relationship to the created order.

Catholic teaching on creation is the only adequate foundation for *response* to creation that is fully aligned with Truth. The true steward of creation is man redeemed by Christ, fed by His own being, sustained in His Body, ordered toward the expectation of a new heavens, new earth and eternity with God. Creation is, thus, much more than 'nature,' or 'the environment,' or the material world. Only in that larger context can the human person find his place as its knower, steward, and re-presenter.

A Catholic understanding of man's relationship to Creation is central to the self-awareness from which our culture springs. Distortion in this understanding distances us from the radiant beauty of the world, from our own rootedness in reality, from our neighbors who are frightened about environmental damage, and from our own capacity for excellence in stewardship and right use of the goods of creation. Benjamin Wiker, in *In Defense of Nature*, considers some of the central environmental questions from the perspective that the created order cannot be divorced from the moral order.

> Very few take the astounding position that there is both a natural ecology and a moral ecology, and that these two are intimately interdependent. ...that is, in fact, the Catholic Church's position, and it has been for two thousand years. ...there is now both significant natural and moral pollution, and they both have a single cause: the human will running roughshod over nature in one way or another. ...

> moral pollution and environmental pollution are inextricably linked. This is necessarily the case because human nature is part of nature, even while it transcends nature. [165]

Stratford Caldecott, in *The Radiance of Being*, also indicates that the human person must be re-placed at the center of this sphere of culture.

> [St. Pope] John Paul affirmed a mystical bond between ourselves and the rest of creation, and sought to recall us to our original mission as stewards and priests of nature, receiving the creation from God's hand, cultivating it or making it fruitful, and giving it back to him in sacrificial worship. The healing of the world around us, he believed, depends on a re-ordering and a healing of the inner world of imagination, intelligence, and will. Man was intended to be the mediator of creation, the one in whom all things connect, through whom all things are reconciled, the image of the invisible God...[166]

> Pope Benedict XVI picked up John Paul's cosmic personalism in *Caritas in Veritate*, which anchors its whole argument in the 'centrality of the human person' (CV, 47) and the relational nature of man (CV, 53-5). For both popes, in fact, 'human ecology' is inseparable from environmental ecology, because respect for ourselves, for our sexuality, and for human life in all its stages and manifestations, is the

---

[165] Benjamin Wiker, *In Defense of Nature*, pg. 8
[166] Stratford Caldecott, *The Radiance of Being*, pg. 85

> manifestation of a respect for nature as such, which has been created in divine Wisdom...[167]

> Without 'the greater hope' that Christianity offers, environmentalism will end in fanaticism or despair.....restriction of Christianity to the individual level is, I take it, precisely what we now need to overcome.[168]

Because many environmental activists accept premises that lead to a hygienist, or anti-life, population-control agenda, Catholics are understandably wary of the whole 'green movement,' and its various assertions and proposals. Fr. Lorenzo Albacete cautions against a religious position that avoids the tension of the Catholic *via media*:

> The dominant culture teaches us that God's presence is not, so to speak, naturally evoked by earthly realities. If God's presence is to be part of human life, it must be forced into it by a sheer act of the will. In this view of things, we don't discover ourselves through engagement with others and the environment. Instead, we construct our identity by forcing the environment to allow space for it. Hostility to environmentalism and environmentalist hostility to human development both originate in this religious position. The former rejects the presence of the sacred in nature, the latter sacralizes it. In any case, when the two are considered at odds, the 'goodness' of a way of life is measured by the achievements of the

---

[167] Stratford Caldecott, *The Radiance of Being*, pg. 86
[168] Stratford Caldecott, *The Radiance of Being*, pg. 91

> person struggling against a depersonalizing environment, rather than discovering a quality inherent in the world outside of us. By force of will we accomplish our successes rather than by being drawn out by the beauty and goodness of what is 'other'.[169]

Science developed from the hunger that stems from the innate religious sense in man, to know, to take in all the reality of the created order. Though science flourished in the medieval historic period of peak integration of Christianity and culture, its relationship to man's inherent desire for God dates back to the Garden of Eden. Man's work of knowing and taking in the world was made arduous by sin, but was still essential to his being. As his fallen nature expressed itself more and more fully in the disorders of pagan culture, his yearning toward God's provision of a way back to wholeness and order continued to grow and to be fed by the reality of the presence of this order in the natural world. Creation yearned for man's reconciliation with God, as it was through man that its full realization was meant to come. Man is the end, or destiny of Creation as Heaven is the end, or destiny of man, Creation's knower, and its lover. These destinies are meant to be fully realized, in the unity, beauty, truth and goodness of the new heavens and new earth which will emerge at the end of time through the consummation of God's union with His bride, the Church.

An approach to Creation taken out of the context of Creation's origin and destiny is reduced, or flattened, and so flattens and reduces the human person. Science and technology abstracted from the human person endanger him, even as they bring positive new developments for his

---

[169] Lorenzo Albacete, *God at the Ritz*, pg. 147

welfare. Catholic faith points the way toward an integral ecology that corresponds to the full reality of man as a physical, intellectual, emotional, moral, relational and spiritual being. Our way leads from the sanctity of life, through worship in community, unity in dialogue, creativity in economics and artistic expression to a recovery of harmony in relationship with Creation.

Creation is ultimately a communication from God about Himself. He is the Reality that calls out to us through creation, that shines forth from within creation, and that presses His claim upon us through the demands and laws of creation. In worship we return time and space and created things such as wine, wheat, gold, wood, and marble to Him as a response to this claim. The radiance draws us toward His beauty. The reverberation of His voice draws us toward all Truth. Until and unless we understand creation as a general communication of God's own being, we will not stand in right relationship to its particulars, or to our own selves.

Catholics can make contributions to this sphere of culture by becoming growers and regenerators of soil, by entering into scientific work with awe and wonder, by examining the fruits of the reductionist/materialist medical model, by humanizing the use of technologies, by struggling to consider environmental issues from multiple perspectives, by placing interest in and learning more about creatures and health and land. Raise and butcher your own pig, view constellations through a telescope, improve your microbiome or regenerate your soil, start a nature journal, support local farmers, contemplate a murmuration of birds, or an octopus solving complex puzzles. Be amazed!

As you allow Creation to speak to you, to move you, to influence you toward its Creator, you will increase your capacity for Christ, and your ability to communicate Him.

**The Sphere of Economics**[170]

Economics is a vital human concern. Many definitions of 'economics' are possible, but they all have to do with the means of generating, conserving and sharing human goods such as vital communities, food, shelter, tools, artworks, education, technologies, clothing, information, natural resources, wisdom, and cultural expressions. This focus on all created and man-made wealth as means to the greater end of the common good of human persons emerges from the Catholic, sacramental, incarnational understanding of reality.

The movement of wealth through mediating structures characterizes economics as a dynamic and exciting field of human endeavor and cultural initiative. Because we are concerned with integral human development, we do not separate goods into categories such as financial, physical, intellectual, aesthetic, spiritual, or necessary and superfluous, or even primary, secondary, tertiary. Rather, we want all possible good for our fellow man, who cannot be reduced to a complex of needs, but rightly seeks and rightly has been given by God all goods in common with us in a gratuitous, magnanimous gesture of love by which God wants to draw us all to himself for our fulfillment and joy.

---

[170] The material in The Sphere of Economics is replicated, to some extent, in my unpublished mss, *Souls at Play*.

Our thoughts about the human person and his needs, our view of our relationship to Creation, our sense of responsibility to and for others, and our understanding of the ownership rights over the goods and skills we possess and make all relate to this sphere of life-in-common with our fellow man. As recipients of the riches of God's grace, we should understand ourselves as having a key role to play in making decisions and adjustments that maximize the cultural wealth in the *oikos*, or households we inhabit. Interest in Economics is interest in what it means to be a channel of grace, to create social capital, and to participate in creative justice.

*Oiko-nomia* – literally, "the law governing the household" – gives rise to the entire cultural sphere of Economics. The Church, in its way, is an economic form. The people of God participate in His sacramental economy – the Resource of all resources: the Eucharist. There are rules and laws concerning its distribution, and a vast network of persons, lit by the "nodes," or "hubs" where priests "transform raw material" and "add value" before "distribution channels" operate to move the Person of Christ into the wider world. All of us exist within the "household" of God's own being and within the shared Creation – an economy of His grace and provision, law and means of distribution, exchange, and interdependent relationships that serves to support human being.

Each of our homes is a small "economic system," operating to provide for the needs of, increase the wealth of, and order the contributions of its members. Economics, understood in the wholeness of human relations, is a much richer conception than the mere "science of exchange and distribution of goods," or "study of wealth creation and exchange," though it certainly encompasses narrower definitions of economics as a subject of academic study.

**Catholic Foundations**

The human person must be returned to the center of the meaning of a form – such as a sphere of culture, an institution, or a conversation – to rightly order its development. The Catholic Catechism refers to man as the author, center and goal of all economic and social life.[171] ... the *human person* ...is and ought to be the principle, the subject and the end of all social institutions.[172] Contrasting this Catholic, personalist approach with the world's reductionist, individualist approach to Economics, Stratford Caldecott cautions us:

> The model of *homo economicus* that we inherit from the Enlightenment was based on man understood as an individual rather than as a "person" in the relational sense. It turns man into a solitary and conflictual actor in the market, an isolated and docile subject of the state, pursuing his own survival, pleasure, and power.[173]

*Caritas in Veritate* addresses the sphere of civil life with its economic and social developments. It offers an excellent overview of the expanded, Catholic perspective of economics as ordered toward fully integral human development, the law of the gift, true wealth building,

---

[171] *Catechism of the Catholic Church*, paragraph 2459
[172] *Gaudium et spes*, 250
[173] Stratford Caldecott, *Not as the World Gives*, pg. 189

social justice and environmental stewardship. Those looking to redeem the culture will be stimulated by the "altogether new and creative challenge" of infusing civilization with love, truth, hope and the logic of the gift of self.

In this encyclical Pope Benedict XVI considers the false dichotomy between "individual" and "institutional" action, stressing that man rightly operates through the institutions he creates, but may not relinquish his responsibility for moral action to those clubs, schools, unions, foundations, corporations, charities and other organizations. They are instruments of human freedom, ruled ultimately by the virtue and freedom of the persons who create and use them.[174] Economics is not a zone of monetary exchange, detached from personal interactions, but is necessarily relational, involving all of the actual, interpersonal, shared life implied in the word "household".

**Economics Makes Good Use of Human Institutions**

G. K. Chesterton said that "Free men always create institutions." Jeff Mirus reinforces the idea that civic life – society as *oikos*, or household, best managed to support and enrich human being – is the necessary "middle place" where the Church meets the world through her lay members and their institutions and activities.

> ...once again I call for the formation and strengthening of culture through "intermediary institutions". ...As a social being, the human person flourishes to the highest degree in a cultural

---

[174] See Caritas in Veritate, 17

> environment in which a wide range of legitimate human interests and ends are pursued cooperatively to achieve a higher level of perfection than the individual can typically achieve on his own, and to influence and enrich the larger culture as a whole. Typically, such cooperative efforts give rise to what we call *intermediary institutions*, cooperative agencies of human organization which – through their own particular excellence, effectiveness and earned respect in a particular field of human endeavor – exercise a powerful influence on how individual persons pursue certain goals, the boundaries and standards applicable to those pursuits, and the responsibilities inherent in them. [175]

A robust network of association and purpose is the key to cultural evangelization, or redemption of culture.

**Logos, Liberty and Leisure**

The highest "good" obtainable in the economic order – the free human person – requires that work be rightly related to worship. Work serves man's freedom when, through it, he raises Creation and raises himself to God in a gesture of gratitude for the gift of his own life. Once again we see that no sphere of cultural activity can be abstracted from the religious sense, the reality of dependence upon God that is of the essence of man's being.

---

[175] Jeff Mirus, "Intermediary Institutions Represent, Preserve and Shape a Robust Culture," http://www.catholicculture.org/commentary/otc.cfm?id=993&repos

"Work is for man, not man for work."[176] *Laborem Exercens* – St. Pope John Paul's elaboration of the Catholic meaning of work – considers work because "it is at the very center of" and "the essential key to" the social question,[177] and thus of the Church's "concept of man and life in society, and, especially the social morality which she worked out according to the needs of different ages."[178]

Work is a fundamental dimension of man's existence.[179] Work is a "transitive" activity, good for the making of the person doing work, and not valuable only for the end products produced.[180] Man's dominion over the earth is achieved by means of work.[181] The proper subject of work is man, conscious and free.[182] Different sorts of work are judged "by the measure of the dignity of" the worker.[183] Through work, man "achieves fulfillment as a human being.[184] Societal structures based upon disordered, reduced, or false understanding of the human person serve to diminish him, thus counteracting the highest *end* of economics: supporting human freedom. Man, subordinated to the goals of profit, production, machine efficiency, is man under the rule of mammon, a false god.

In *Leisure, the Basis of Culture*, Josef Pieper asks, "can we not see what it means for there to be an institution in

---

[176] *Catechism of the Catholic Church*, paragraph 2428, citing *Laborem Exercens* 6
[177] *Laborem Exercens* 2
[178] *Laborem Exercens* 3
[179] *Laborem Exercens* 6
[180] *Laborem Exercens* 4
[181] *Laborem Exercens* 5
[182] *Laborem Exercens* 5, 6
[183] *Laborem Exercens* 6
[184] *Laborem Exercens* 9

the world that prohibits useful actions, or the 'servile arts' on certain days, and thus prepares space for a non-proletarian existence?"[185] He first established that leisure keeps us human, and then warned that leisure separated from worship becomes inhuman. Like Pope Benedict XVI, Pieper sees the necessary corrective for the inhumanity of the economic, or civic, sphere of human culture in the higher order of eternal reality, Holy Wisdom, and Trinitarian love.

In *Not as the World Gives*, Stratford Caldecott reflects on and expands upon *Caritas in Veritate*, making it clear that the battle for man is a war of words, of *logos*, or logic.

> The errors of modernity are spiritually based, and will not be rooted out easily. But should we be surprised at this? The "Battle of the Logos" was foreseen in the Book of Revelation. The Battle is described in the most graphic way in the Book of Revelation (19:11-21), where the Word of God, clad in robes dipped in blood, rides out to war, his eyes like a flame of fire. "From his mouth issues a sharp sword with which to smite the nations, and he will rule them with a rod of iron; he will tread the winepress of the fury of the wrath of God the Almighty." The Founder of Christianity, after all, is on record as saying he came not to bring peace but a sword (Mt 10:34-6). The sword is an instrument of division, of opposition. Sword implies Battle.[186]

How might Love's logic inform the world of business, work, and trade in goods and services? There are many possible creative Catholic responses to this question.

---

[185] Josef Pieper, *Leisure, the Basis of Culture*
[186] Stratford Caldecott, *Not As the World Gives*, pg. 79

In each case, the power of modeling – lived, real-life examples of ideas realized in various actual forms – allows many more people to interact with Catholic ideas than will ever explore those ideas in writing, or conversation. The direct encounter with Catholic principles in action is itself an invitation to the humanity, freedom, and creativity of those who see completely new possibilities made manifest.

One influential model is the Economics of Communion, developed by the Focolare movement (officially known to the Vatican as The Work of Mary). Foundress Chiara Lubich influenced the development of this beautifully creative and effective approach to the infusion of gratuitousness into economic institutions in our times. There is a great deal more to be learned about Economics of Communion (at least one Catholic college now offers a doctoral program in this specialty), but her thoughts may stimulate your own creativity in the economic order.

> The aim of the Economy of Communion…is an economy that has to do with communion among people and with the sharing of goods….we often use these words that appear beautiful to us: the "culture of giving." … It does not always mean depriving ourselves of something in order to give it away. In reality, these words stand for…the culture of love….the human person …finds fulfillment precisely in loving, in giving. This need to love lies in the deepest core of our being, whether we are believers or not. …The project of the Economy of Communion, however,

does not ask us to love only the needy, but everyone. The spirituality of unity demands it. Therefore, it asks that we love all those who in one way or another are involved in the business. For example, I wrote: "Let's give always: give a smile, understanding, forgiveness, our listening; let's give our intelligence, our will and our availability; let's give our experiences and skills. Give: let this be word that gives us no rest."…we see the need for the Economy of Communion to have and to help develop "new men and women."… the laity must become holy where they are, in the world. …they are called to Christianize (renew with the gospel) the various spheres of human society, by their personal witness and by the spoken word… we feel the urgent need to open schools for entrepreneurs, economists, teachers and students of economics, for all sectors of business…Indeed, we should feel called to transform every hour of our workday into a masterpiece of precision, or order and of harmony….those who work in the Economy of Communion are called to make themselves one with each individual and with the collectivity they serve; in other words, to work in such a way that everything done by their hands may be love.[187]

---

[187] Chiara Lubich, "The Charism of Unity and the Economy," in *Essential Writings: Spirituality, Dialogue, Culture*, pg. 278-288. See also Lorna Gold, "From Spirituality of Communion to "Economy of Communion": The Evolution of a New Economic Culture" in Jesus Christ, the New Face of Social Progress, pg. 193-226, Peter Casarella, editor. The book *Jesus Christ, the New Face of Social Progress* is a collection of essays by Catholics in response to Pope Benedict's 2009 encyclical *Caritas in Veritate* – all explaining "how an encounter with the person of Jesus Christ is the true basis for economic and social progress."

Are you surprised to hear the words "love," "communion," and "giving" in a discussion of business, profit, economic reality and work?

To renew the sphere of Economics we need not be expert economists, but actors, vitally interested in the economic order as rich in possibilities for cultural expression of our deepest beliefs and values. Faith filled work has the potential to generate an evangelistic context that helps our fellow man develop greater capacity to receive the proclamation of the Good News as he answers God's call to develop his own freedom. Far from being "about money, jobs, and greed," economics has proven to be "about" freedom, mercy, justice, creativity and love.

Economics should certainly not be dismissed as "merely materialistic," though it involves us intimately in the material world and the material needs of our fellow man. Our works of mercy, communion-inspired businesses and institutions, and our growing holiness all speak the same 'language' – the Love we proclaim has entered history in the flesh to establish an economy of grace. Speaking of Catholics' tendency to "remain aloof from things of material concern," Father Benedict Groeschel gave some solid advice:

> A person interested in spiritual growth must overcome the tendency to remain aloof from things of material concern. He or she should nourish a constant, dedicated interest in those who suffer from injustice. The more one can directly associate with the victims of injustice, share their lot, plead their cause and defend them, the more one will grow spiritually.[188]

---

[188] *Spiritual Passages*, Groeschel, Crossroad, NY, 1984, pg. 159

## The Sphere of Education

We first prepare for making contributions in every sphere of culture by immersion in them, in the family and community, and in the Liturgy. Once we reach the age of conscious co-operation in the work of learning, we enter the sphere of formal education. The effortless (though sometimes painful) work of constant encounter with and response to reality, scientific discovery and experimentation, cyclical movement in time and ritual, immersive language learning, music and proprioception has made us ready for the less direct and effort-ful work of learning through abstraction, symbol, concept and imaginal dis-placement of Self into other worlds, times and perspectives.

Context and community – rich learning environments – have prepared us for 'content,' but education must go beyond mere information transfer if it is to serve the human person at its center. Once again, the 'going beyond' is a function of love, as in work turned to Art, Creation realized through man, and the Economics of grace and gift. The intransitive value of all man's working is the making of the human person. In the sphere of Art, man speaks love through form. In the sphere of Creation, man receives love through form. In Economics, man sets form a-speaking through exchange and gift. In Education, teachers set form a-growing through life-to-life transfer.

The art of teaching is the art of making what is enormous and real in yourself into a form small enough to be communicated *to* and *for* a person without the capacity for the wholeness of that reality. The stewardship of teaching is to cultivate the skills and faculties of the human person, tending to the richness of the soil and responding to the changing needs of his growing up. The economics of teaching involves the condescension of love to meet one who needs what you possess, and the incorporation of knowledge into forms that build into structures which hold value over time and place. As in every sphere, all may be found in the one you have in focus.

Education involves us in forms, such as teaching models, textbooks, testing requirements, scope-and-sequences, school calendars, transcripts, course outlines, curriculum committees, and school buildings, which all are in-formed by philosophy, history, understanding of the human person, and resolutions to many tensions that, once resolved, may not be apparent in the final forms. For example, many resolutions of tension are embodied in the decision to place a Drawing class in the regular or extracurricular schedule, how much time to give it, whether to make it a requirement or an elective, whether to use John Ruskin's approach,[189] or the more contemporary *Drawing on the Right Side of the Brain*,[190] and on what basis to give students a grade.

Models evolve so that each of hundreds of decisions need not be made again and again, but sometimes obscure the questions they answer, and the opportunity costs of sticking to one or another collection of answers. Just as habits develop from repeated neural patterns which connect and smooth many related decisions and movements, "the way we've always done it" develops in every sphere of human activity as a form that is easier to accept than to re-think. Awareness that it is a form can help you look through it to the meanings, questions and answers it embodies, and

---

[189] See: John Ruskin, *The Elements of Drawing*
[190] See: Betty Edwards, *Drawing on the Right Side of the Brain*

consider changes if it is not working toward the freedom of the persons 'inside' the form.

That awareness can also help you to appreciate the enormity of carving one path out of a wilderness of possible paths through a territory, whether the territory is 'Biology 101,' or 'responding to the culture'. You will be less likely to throw out one educational model and start over with a new one if you respect that a re-formation must involve communication about the questions and tensions that underlie whatever form is chosen. G.K. Chesterton had decided opinions about reformers that simply tear down established forms:

> In the matter of reforming things, as distinct from deforming them, there is one plain and simple principle; a principle which will probably be called a paradox. There exists in such a case a certain institution or law; let us say, for the sake of simplicity, a fence or gate erected across a road. The more modern type of reformer goes gaily up to it and says, "I don't see the use of this; let us clear it away." To which the more intelligent type of reformer will do well to answer: "If you don't see the use of it, I certainly won't let you clear it away. Go away and think. Then, when you can come back and tell me that you do see the use of it, I may allow you to destroy it.

The two-way perspective of Catholic communication also indicates an approach to education that is community-based and multi-directional. The free, acting human person perceives education as a delight and as something enjoyable to share with other persons. We can educate one another in our areas of special interest, so as to multiply the investment we each make in our own continuing education. Some of us may thus make difficult Catholic material more accessible and widely known, or share with others the access our own expertise grants to areas of thought now often sequestered in ivory towers. For instance, we might exchange book digests, offer seminars, convene book study groups, create great explainer videos, or just share great quotes and articles with friends. Skill-sharing strengthens the whole community to grow and can vegetables, raise and feed a family, take responsibility for health and fitness, save money by doing repairs, or live through trauma and hard times. What do you possess that you could teach others for love of Christ?

Chapter 11

# The Possibilities of Form

Whether we call it 'evangelization,' or 'contributing to the cultural conversation,' or 'co-operating with God in our own becoming,' form-making involves us in 'speaking truth in love' (acting, building verbal structures, sculpting institutions, composing symphonic conversations). To communicate Christ in new forms is the highest possibility of attending to our own and others' integral development, as *Caritas in Veritate* refers to the whole-person-centered approach to every sphere of culture. Form-making calls upon your intellectual and imaginative capacity, in addition to the specific skills your medium requires.

**Innovation, Creativity, Generativity**

The innovative human being is celebrated and sought after. In recognition of the oppressive nature of the machine as a model for the workplace, and the human cost to workers of the industrial revolution, many contemporary voices are calling for attention to the role of imagination and creativity in building a better world. Innovation in business is one of the most-studied developments of our time. The corporate world is making adjustments to a constantly changing global landscape and to an increasingly participatory social environment. Competitive advantage is the primary good sought by innovators, but there is also increasing demand for human goods such as flexible schedules, online working from home, extended parental leave, employee ownership and governance, and employee 'perks' that range from nap pods to on-site daycare to concierge services and financial planning assistance.

As the practices of notably innovative companies such as Google, Apple, Zappos, 3M and Pixar become widely known (via a growing body of popular literature about the topic of business innovation, and via TED talks and the companies' own social media outreach), employees everywhere develop higher expectations for the workplace to be a humanly satisfying physical and social environment, and for their work to pay off in more than material satisfaction. A handful of stand-out models re-set the bar of expectation for everyone.

The language of innovation is often marked by the Zen Buddhism which has influenced a significant cultural shift away from materialism and mechanistic organizational structures in the economic culture. Catholics can value the emphasis on deep restedness and recollection, humble questioning and willingness to learn, aware presence to the factors of reality, and elegant simplicity that are promoted as paths toward creative problem solving and innovation. Inventiveness, flexibility of thought, and a creative approach to problem solving can also be taught, which is changing the approach to education in interesting new ways. This is another area for fruitful dialogue with secular culture.

We can learn from innovative, hybrid enterprises about promoting a free-flow of ideas, encouraging horizontal interactions among diverse members/employees, creating spaces that foster conversation, investing in failure, taking risks, and cultivating diverse, resilient networks. We'll surely find valuable insights in our own Church history to share with a culture that is genuinely interested in casting a wide net for 'input'. For example, Chris Lowney's book *Heroic Leadership* makes current and accessible to a modern audience the leadership principles of St. Ignatius of Loyola (founder of the Society of Jesus) and his culture-building 'company' of highly innovative, resourceful, and courageous actors. "Innovation and creativity happen when individuals enjoy a wide berth and the managerial support to take risks," says Lowney.[191]

**Creativity**

Innovation and creativity flourish in organizations that make time, space, and a supportive culture for their demands:

> For innovation to flourish, it has to be seen as an integral purpose of the whole organization rather than as a separate function. ...Innovation is the child of imagination. Nourishing imagination is an essential part of growing a culture of innovation. A good deal of creative work, especially in the early stages of a project, is about openly playing with ideas, riffing, doodling, improvising and exploring new possibilities.... Creativity loves collaboration. ...Creative cultures are inquiring. Innovation involves trial and error, being wrong at times and sometimes having to back up and start again.[192]

---

[191] Chris Lowney, *Heroic Leadership*
[192] Ken Robinson, *Out of Our Minds*

> ...design thinking is embodied thinking – embodied in teams and projects, to be sure, but embodied in the physical spaces of innovation as well. ...The project spaces are large enough that the accumulated research materials, photos, storyboards, concepts, and prototypes can be out and available all of the time.[193]

The paradox of innovation is that the organizations emphasize order and control, and yet improvisation seems to be uncontrollable. The manager of a traditional team is responsible for breaking down the task, keeping everyone on schedule, and coordinating the team members. But the leader of a collaborative team couldn't be more different; this leader has to establish creative spaces within which group genius is more likely to happen. Because innovative teams are self-managing, the leader doesn't have as much direct managerial work to do. Instead, leaders of innovative groups are active participants in the work; they function more like a peer than a boss.[194]

We need to be willing to risk embarrassment, ask silly questions, surround ourselves with people who don't know what we're talking about. We need to leave behind the safety of our expertise.[195]

Creativity is a step further on from imagination. Imagination can be an entirely private process

---

[193] Tim Brown, *Change by Design*
[194] Kenneth Sawyer, *Group Genius*
[195] Jonah Lehrer, *Imagine*

of internal consciousness. ...Being creative involves doing something...People are not creative in the abstract...Creativity involves putting your imagination to work. In a sense, creativity is applied imagination. Innovation is the process of putting new ideas into practice. Innovation is applied creativity...Innovation is always about introducing something new, or improved, or both, and it is usually assumed to be a positive thing.[196]

Creativity involves the resolution of elements in tension. The tension may take the form of a problem statement, a design brief, an articulation of competing realities, an intentional juxtaposition meant to draw out new connections, or a new idea persons desire to see realized. The resolution may take the form of a novel approach, an invention, a new use for an old form, a surprising response, a new work of art, or a verbal structure – simple as a request for forgiveness, or complex as a knowledge management protocol, or constitution.

## Generativity

Generativity is a further development made possible by unity and collaboration with others. Though 'horizontal' teamwork accounts for a lot of innovation and creativity, the 'something more' implied by the word 'generativity' is a kind of fruitfulness that makes your form a vessel for 'vertical' infusion of power from above the material and even the intellectual plane. The form you make may have power, itself, to generate, or inspire, or give rise to

---

[196] Ken Robinson, *Out of Our Minds*

further form. While someone might invent a destructive technology, or create an 'ode to the culture of death,' generativity refers to life-giving form that expands to support and promote life, or the life of derivative forms.

Practice is needed to develop your receptive capacity for form, your verbal, metaphorical and sacramental dimensions, your responsive power, your core and extension strength, your ability to place yourself into heartfelt, prayerful, intentional, Spirit-filled unity with Others, your humility and docility, your intellectual and imaginative faculties, your freedom and self-awareness. You can learn to take an innovative approach, think like a designer, work like a craftsman, resolve tension creatively, and to generate 'teaching seeds,' truth-in-charity forms, and excellent mediating structures. As you learn, you'll practice at failing forward, praying for help, and, as Mother Angelica said, "doing the ridiculous so that God can do the impossible."

In the same way that 'person' is generated in free act (in the practice of freedom), 'community' is generated in acts-in-unity (in the work we do together, in unity). If *being* the Body of Christ is essential to communicating Christ, then collaboration in the work of communicating Christ is essential to becoming Christ-in-His-Church. Scripture says the people we need to reach will know our identity is Christ by our love for one another. 'They' will perceive that love as 'we' turn toward them, together.[197] The form of our unity and the forms we create in that unity become invitations to freedom in Christ to the extent they are carried to others on the generative wings of Love.

---

[197] John 13:35: "By this everyone will know that you are my disciples, if you love one another."

'Generation' implies not only the quickening to new life of a form, (as when the life of Christ is given through Baptismal grace), but also its fuller realization, or maturation (as in "working out your salvation,"[198] or co-operating with grace). A form which is 'generated' needs allowance of time and space for its organic growth. Products can be made on a linear conveyor belt, but living forms participate in a spiral, recursive pattern of movement which derives from the back-and-forth, lemniscate movement of the Holy Spirit. Creativity can be said to 'add' one thing to another, while generativity 'multiplies'. Living faith blooms, or grows, or emerges into a hope-fullness that is a life-giving context.

## Generating the Context of Hope

Hope is a theological virtue that, like Faith and Love, is a pure gift from God. It is also the quality, or atmosphere, of the Way that rejoins, reweaves and reconciles the 'missing middles' we find in the social fabric, the polarized civil sphere, the flattened human person, and the culture of death. The work of communication is a 'middlework' with enormous potential to generate a force that dispels despair like light dispels darkness. That force is hope.

J. R. R. Tolkien's Elves had two words for hope: *amdir* which indicated the 'looking up' of optimism, and *estel* which was the greater hope in the *being* of things that we would call 'trust' in God.[199] Whereas the infused virtue is

---

[198] Philippians 2:12: "work out your own salvation with fear and trembling."

[199] This connects to Pieper's discussion of the roots of festivity in *In Tune with the World* – affirmation of the goodness of things from which springs true worship.

pure gift, the hope that radiates from our trust in God is rather like a disposition to receive the gift. As sacramentals (blessed objects) help dispose us to receive grace, acts of faith fill the world's 'gaps' with the sort of "world-mothering air" that poet Gerard Manley Hopkins perceived in Mary's devotion to those for whom her Son died.[200] A vacuum cannot support life, but the hope-filled atmosphere radiating from our hope-full forms can.

Hope is the context in which the sound of love resounds. If the word were a seed, hope would be the ground, the place-within-which the seed opens to become fully itself. The space of hope is held coherent-and-open by the forms that express Faith and invite Love's power into vessels of persons, materials, words, and memory. The 'structure' of hope may seem invisible, like a mother, to the children of this world. The sons and daughters of God, though, perceive its substance and strength. In the "post-Christian" era, we see as never before that people can inhabit the same spatial-temporal and social places, yet live in completely different universes of meaning, depending on what informs their beliefs about reality.

Hope has collapsed for many of the people right beside us. The rich atmosphere of Christian culture has been largely destroyed, leaving man gasping for breath in a culture of death hardly habitable for human beings. We must do more than speak true words about Jesus in this vacuum. We must reweave the chamber, the place wherein word may reverberate. For us, the Church is a huge vessel of hope – context within context: liturgy within sacred time within cathedral within international church within history. We are

---

[200] Gerard Manley Hopkins, "The Blessed Virgin Compared to the Air We Breathe"

held, boundaried, enwombed, supported in our hope-rich chamber and able to breathe freely. But not all have the strength left even to draw near, much less to enter. We dare not abandon the Ark to reach them, and yet we must rescue the perishing.

Where we perceive ourselves as living, moving and having being in God, the Enlightenment project has successfully convinced most people they live only in their own disconnected minds. Many even question the realities of Self and Other, Creation and morality, freedom and purpose. Encounter with reality is buffered by labels, mental constructs, and technologies that deaden our capacity to sense and respond to it. Abstracted from home, family, our bodies, nature, community – foundational realities for the *becoming* of integrated human persons – the Self withers and becomes less and less able to encounter reality, to generate a judgment, to resound in freedom.

The Enlightenment 'god' says "You will be more and more free as all the baggage of religion, history, mythos, ritual, and material are stripped away." The Triune and only God says "You will be more and more free as you are surrounded by and receptive to substance filled with significance." Post-Christian culture is marked by *contempt for means* of grace and for mediating structures. That contempt diminishes the idea of 'person,' and has contributed to the erosion of the matrix of hope that should surround and support free human being. The lack of poetic depth, capacity for nuance, analogical sense, or metaphorical dimension even in Catholics has left the Church weakened to build community and to make new forms.

Creation is emptied of the sound of God calling and of the radiance of His glory by rationalist, reductionist, materialist 'science' bereft of Wisdom. It seems most people have blindly accepted the Enlightenment presumption that reality is inert. But God *is* Reality, exerting Himself to call to us, to move us to come to Him. St. Peter walked on water because faith is substantial – *more* real than water – not an impotent abstraction. Abstraction leads to despair. We are designed to need means, substance, mediating structures, actuality, and the certainty that God is a real person who loves us.

The atmosphere around us is thin, the ground despoiled, the silence crushing. We need some way to bridge that chasm. Words (persons, forms, works of art, acts) are the means. Your acts of freedom expand your freedom by generating a support matrix for freedom – the scaffolding holding open the hope of Heaven for all who enter not only the Church, but your forms, your presence, your home, and the gravitational pull of your being. Faith is substantial. It is not an idea about God, but the very substance of knowing Him, which flowers into hope and reaches out toward the Love who placed it within you.

"Sustained by the Spirit, communicate hope," said St. Pope John Paul. "The Spirit is the guardian of hope in the human heart. ...Christian communicators will communicate hope credibly if they first experience hope in their own lives, and this will happen only if they are men and women of prayer. ...They must be schooled in hope by the Holy Spirit, the principal agent of the new evangelization, so that they can communicate hope to others."[201] It is a work of mercy to communicate Christ. Your words and forms become mercy-filled as you become mercy-saturated, dwelling in the Ocean of Mercy – context and content of Love.

---

[201] St. Pope John Paul II, Message for the 32nd World Communications Day

The world is full of lies, the un-making of man, persons in bondage, and vain imaginations. We fight against that by filling the world with truth, free human beings, community, affirmation of reality, acts of mercy, courage and fearlessness, worship and praise, works of beauty and integrity, and reasons for hope. The structure of the Kingdom of God is emerging – like a ship through fog, and like Christ moving through the closed door of the upper room – right *through* the realities that obscure it – because it is *more* substantial.[202]

Your forms are meant to convey something of this invisible-but-substantial structure. Small and seemingly insignificant as they may be, they will challenge and confront and do battle with lies by virtue of Truth's inaudible-but-powerful sound. Your desire to communicate Christ will be realized in whatever forms, acts, gestures, words, structures, or relationships you create, to the extent they correspond to the Reality of God. That 'extent' is a complex function of your freedom and virtue, trust and faith, skill and opportunity, intention and love, and the integrity and truth of your forms themselves.

**What, Then, Shall We Make?**

Before us is the possibility of collaborating as the Body of Christ to communicate Christ in new forms. With the Liturgical, social, and organizational work of the Church, our innovative, creative, and generative activities should help reweave the social fabric – community and other structures that support human becoming – so that the growth and integral development of free human persons

---

[202] Thanks to C.S. Lewis for this image of the super-reality of Jesus.

is lifted up to draw all men closer to Christ. You already are 'making forms' as you converse, live family life, grow businesses, and show hospitality. People of the Word, offered as *means* for God's communication of Himself to man, generate a context of hope – like a hot wire with an electro-magnetic field around it – within which the Word may dwell richly and resound. Wherever you are led to respond to the realities you encounter, you will do more.

You will refill empty signs, plant trustworthy seeds in rich soil, build invisible infrastructure for freedom, conserve values in institutions, liberate resources through new mediating structures, voice paths through wilderness and shine light upon the texture of reality that seems impermeable. You will educate others, share the fruits of your intellectual life, teach skills and traditions, write travel guides and course outlines to lead others on journeys, slay giants and rescue the perishing.

You will learn from trees how to convert inanimate minerals into living food, and how to develop vast, resilient networks of communication. You'll learn from fractals and foam how to grow in dimension, distribute goods efficiently, and in-fill territory effectively. You'll learn from the human body how to limit self-defense, listen 'vertically' and 'horizontally' like the heart, expand receptive surface area like the lungs, strengthen bones with action for freedom, and resonate with the full spectrum of reality like the vagus nerve. You'll give tastes of truth to whet and cultivate appetite for truth, glimpses of beauty to lure interest beyond the veil, and simple melodies to prepare the way for symphonies. You'll tell new and excellent stories, challenge those who destroy definitions, insist on hierarchies of value, grow in responsive power, and propose objective truths patiently and peacefully.

These are all things words can do, persons can do, forms can do. Rhetoric, remember, is finding the best means of persuasion. The Liturgy is 'rhetoric,' designed by and realized through Christ-in-His-Church. Creation is 'rhetoric' designed by God to be realized through persons. Persons themselves could be called 'arguments,' 'means,' or 'rhetoric' designed by the Creator and realized through their own co-operation. God chose you, chose us, as the best means of persuasion that He *is*, that He has provided a Way of reconciliation, that His law is just and loving and life-giving, and that He is worthy of all glory, honor, and power.

**Ideas for Formation**

Your own forms, and the whole 'body' of work you create over a lifetime, constitute a 'rhetoric,' or 'poetics,' in the sense that they realize, or manifest, what you are 'for' and 'against,' persuasively. You might start by writing your own *Credo* ("I believe"), listing your skills, mind-mapping your networks of affiliation, or keeping a reading list. You might make explainer videos, pecha kucha presentations, third places, digital gardens, skunkworks, TED-like talks, open source classes, podcasts, apprenticeships, substacks, interactive museum exhibits, books that turn into conversations, events that invite others to practice new forms of communication, schools that grow into intergenerational communities, and websites that become playgrounds.

Your forms might strengthen the human biome, regenerate the land, speak truth to power. You might open your home to the lonely, turn your 'friends' into friendships, trade chat for conversation and make real contact with your 'contacts'. You'll realize the value of old forms and invest them with new life. The Sign of the Cross, saint stories, the *Summa Theologia*, encyclicals, choral speech, formal prayer, feast day celebrations, the Liturgy of the Hours, formal courtesies – all are forms that grow empty with inattention, and full with intentionality.

You might awaken interest, provoke self-awareness, or open the windows of a mental bunker by asking good questions. A question is a 'form,' or 'verbal structure' that can start a conversation, build a relationship, elicit stories, and engage the imagination. Neil Postman, in *Teaching as a Conserving Activity*, suggests we "make the study of the art of question-asking one of the central disciplines in language education." "…the form in which a question is asked will control the kind of answer one gets," he says. "A question is a structure for thought." He continues: "Language education, therefore, must include the most serious exploration of the structure of questions – their assumptions, limitations, levels of abstraction, and the sources of authority to which they appeal. Without this knowledge our students can barely be said to know anything."[203]

Questions can be fun ("What topics will get you on your soap box?" "What's the most ridiculous thing you've ever yelled at your kids?" "What are your pet peeves?"), strategic ("What is your most compelling argument for the doctrine that there is no God?" "What could the Church learn from your experience?" "What models should our organization emulate?"), and simple ("What are your interests?" "What 'negative' experience turned out to hold something 'positive'? "What question do you wish others would ask you?"). Just be sure you actually are interested

---

[203] Neil Postman, *Teaching as a Conserving Activity*, pg.156

in hearing the answer. Pose the questions for yourself to answer in a journal, ask a few at the dinner table, or make a list and conduct an interview with someone you admire.

There is a world of 'community conversation' to consider joining, or emulating. Town Meeting, Bohm Dialogue, Citizen Choicework, Conversation Café, and other forms are secular attempts to promote engagement in the civic sphere, strengthen pluralist communities, and encourage participation in politics. "To reclaim conversation, we have to be explicit and make conversation a value at every level of an organization. And in organizations of every size."[204] The terms of engagement in these groups tends to be acceptance of a liberal understanding of the 'neutral' civic sphere, which lauds a plurality of ideas but simultaneously conditions participants to reject religious ideas.[205] Just be aware, and be prepared.

Subscribers to journals such as *Communio* and *The Lamp* gather to discuss the current issue. Writers gather to share work in progress. Cities and universities (or a diocese, a parish?) adopt a community book-of-the-year for widespread reading, to promote citizen discussions. The

---

[204] Sherry Turkle, *Reclaiming Conversation*, pg. 284

[205] "We must expose the con game of liberalism which enables it, precisely without argument, to privilege its place in the public order. We must patiently attempt to bring to light the theological dualism, typically unconscious but for all that still theological in its implication, which shapes liberalism's claim of a purely formal religious freedom. We must do this all the while retrieving the positive value of the freedom liberalism rightly intends to protect. The point is not to deny freedom but to transform it with love: to seek to place freedom within the *communio* which alone finally frees and whose truth, as the truth of love, remains ever and in principle – and not just for temporary or strategic reasons – committed to freedom." David L. Schindler, *Heart of the World, Center of the Church*, pg. 88

Church, as an organization, needs our conversations at every level. What if conversation, intellectual life, faith integration and hope generation could be practiced at a million kitchen tables, in a hundred thousand study circles, literary discussions, and professional/vocational groups? What if we communicate Christ through every form we make?

**New Forms, Old Forms**

Write letters, tweets, blog posts, position papers, speeches, book reviews, or a tourist guide to your beautiful church. Share quotations, tell stories, contribute to magazines, exchange lesson plans. Make memes, infographics, non-profit organizations, a map of pilgrimage sites, online communities, or a database of the sacred art in your diocese. Respond to whatever you read; interview someone you admire; promote the work of an artist; fund cultural initiatives. Other communicators are hungry for your feedback and encouragement! Organize an event: exhibition, prize competition, concert, conference, festival, open meeting, live podcast, panel discussion, flash mob, Jefferson dinner, sing-along, jam session, bowling party, or barn raising. Invite others to learn your skills, or take hope from your journey to wholeness.

It's both overwhelming and exhilarating to consider so many possibilities for practicing communication. Anthony Esolen, in *Out of the Ashes*, considers the enormity of the task of rebuilding culture:

> What shall we do now? The answer is both daunting and liberating. We do everything. That doesn't mean that I do everything, or that you

do everything. Suppose you find yourself in a bombed out city. There are all kinds of things to do, and all of them have to be done. Some needs are more pressing than others, and some things can be done only after other things are in order. But everywhere you turn, there's work to do. You have to find clean water. You have to find food. You have to tend to the wounded and bury the dead. You have to erect shelters. You have to see which of the few buildings left standing are actually safe. You have to demolish those that are ruined beyond repair. You have to organize work teams. Someone has to prepare the meals. Someone has to keep the children out of trouble. In such a situation, it's almost absurd to ask whether it's more important to build a latrine than to gather together some undamaged books. All of it has to be done. So you do what you can do—the work that is ready to your hand.

We are made to matter, to generate form. Do what you can, what you want to, what even one friend wants to join you in doing. Communicate Christ into the world by being and creating form that resounds Him. Do everything! Or, as John Henry Newman suggested, dare to do something.[206]

**Form and Fingerprint**

The mind of man, and the works of man, correspond to the nature of God in Whom all else exists. Dorothy Sayers, in *The Mind of the Maker*, discusses the correspondence

---

[206] "Therein lies the nobility of the Faith: that we have the heart to dare something." Blessed Cardinal John Henry Newman

between the Trinitarian Creator and the human form-maker, and between the artist and his forms.[207] This correspondence allows us to consider the 'Father,' 'Son,' and 'Spirit' aspects, or dimensions, of the forms we create. In our forms, the three dimensions are 'Idea,' 'Energy' (the activity of actualizing the Idea), and 'Power'. The created, manifest, given and received, reconstituted-in-the-recipient *form* is the One Thing these 'three persons' exist together *as*.

The works of a creator are ways of communication between other minds and his. He is known through his works, though he transcends them. The more his Energy moves into the diverse parts of his body of work, the more unity and power the whole will possess. The artist must love and work within the constraints of his medium to work freely. If he escapes from them, or takes 'illegal' liberties, he violates the work. His characters are subordinate to the plot, but also must be accorded some freedom in order to develop. The power of the work, the unity of characters and situation, or Energy and Idea, comes from the extent to which the author pours his Energy into them. He does the work of putting himself in their place, giving himself their minds. The artist sacrifices himself for the life of the form he creates, and that sacrifice is energetic, active, intentional, and essential.

All our works of sub-creation can and should be tested for truth, for structural strength, for balance of Energy, Idea, and Power. Just as we don't want to 'confound the Persons' of the Trinity, we want to keep in mind this Trinitarian structure of created forms to see them more truly. Distinction, justice, or 'against' strength, holds the

---

[207] For more on this correspondence of trinities, see Chapter 8 – The Arts of Communication

elements of a work in opposition, so that the actuality of each one is as important as, and inviolate within, the whole composition. And, just as we don't want to 'divide the substance' of the Trinity, we don't want to forget or violate the unity of form that must characterize the true, excellent, beautiful, virtuous, good, form. Conformation, 'with strength,' integral human development, and artistic truth make of the elements a truly 'new' thing wherever justice meets mercy, or love speaks the truth.

Only the Divine Trinity has a structure we might call an 'equilateral triangle'.[208] Imperfections in the works of human creatures result in what Sayers called 'scalene' structure: defects in the Energy, Idea, and Power of their works. A work that is 'all Father' characterizes "many an unreadable monument of scholarship". A work with defect in its Idea loses its controlling unity, or close-knit intellectual coherence. A work that is 'all Spirit' characterizes "many a column of sob-stuff," the "unliterary writer," or an "inartistic artist". "Men who use words without inspiration and without sympathy" fail in Power or Wisdom. A work that is 'all Son' characterizes "many a whirlwind bustle of incoherent episode". Failures in Energy are characteristic of uncreative, frustrated, and inexpressive artists.

---

[208] It bothered me that an equilateral triangle had 60-degree angles. I wanted the 'God triangle' to be a 'right triangle,' with 90-degree angles – call it a strange, poetic longing. Then I discovered that, in spherical (as opposed to plane) geometry, an equilateral triangle with three 90-degree angles is considered possible. It doesn't change the metaphorical use of a triangle as God's fingerprint in Creation, but it has made this poet happy to feel the 'poetic justice' or rightness of this!

Sayers' caution about the way words, literally, matter, flows from the understanding that the forms we make participate in the creative power of God, for good, or ill:

> ...the Power of the Word...is dangerous. Every word – even every idle word – will be accounted for at the day of judgement, because the word itself has power to bring to judgement. It is of the nature of the word to reveal itself and to incarnate itself – to assume material form. Its judgement is therefore an intellectual, but also a material judgement. The habit, very prevalent today, of dismissing words as "just words" takes no account of their power. But once the Idea has entered into other minds, it will tend to reincarnate itself there with ever-increasing Energy and ever-increasing Power. It may for some time incarnate itself only in more words, more books, more speeches; but the day comes when it incarnates itself in actions, and this is its day of judgement. ...a true act of creation...if it is an evil idea, ...will create, to a large extent by active negation – that is to say, by destruction. The fact...that "all activity is of God" means that no creative Idea can be wholly destructive: some creation will be produced together with the destruction; and it is the work of the creative mind to see that the destruction is redeemed by its creative elements.[209]

Not only do these observations about God's 'fingerprint' in our forms help us to correct, balance, and perfect the forms themselves, but they also point to ways to strengthen

---

[209] Dorothy Sayers, *The Mind of the Maker*, pg. 111, 112

them, and, thus, the human person, who began and now ends this work. We can only improve our communications, our forms, our Selves if we evaluate and learn from flaws and failures. We do not aim for a static perfection, but a dynamic, growing perfection. As we grow up, and as we improve, we'll fail in new ways. We rise as form in the center of a movement of the Holy Spirit, who is the ultimate weaver-together of fulfilled form. The human person is at the chiastic center of God's communication of Himself – he is, because God is, and he becomes, as he communicates Christ.

Chapter 12

# Recapitulation of the Human Person

As promised, we now end by returning to the human person who communicates Christ. You are the teacher, builder, path maker, integrator, mediating structure, responder, storyteller, world weaver, whose every word and act helps to restore the world's wholeness and its capacity to support human becoming. You, acting in freedom and in unity with the Body of Christ, voice His response to the realities you face with Him, and within His Church.

**You are God's Instrument**

It may seem galling to think of God 'using' you. He has, in fact, chosen to work through you. He has, far from instrumentalizing (objectifying, exteriorizing) you, given you an interior dimension through which His Spirit may play, may love, may respond, if you say yes. You are his workmanship, his *poema*, crafted to accomplish His purposes while becoming, in the process, fully alive – fully realized as you.[210]

Your response-ability, plus your smallness, make you just the instrument for changing the world. "The higher the leverage point, the more the system will resist changing

---
[210] Ephesians 2:10

it."[211] The human person who becomes an actor in the enormous 'world system' built of lies confounds it – infusing it with newness of life and hope without causing a demise that crushes those within. The small, even tiny, symbolic free act has within it the radiance of God's glory and the power of your freedom. By every free act, you light the darkness and transmit life-giving love. By every free act, you expand your sphere of response-ability.

If you're feeling overwhelmed by responsibility for all that's wrong with the world, you may be vainly imagining at the wrong scale. Your scale – the human scale – is here, now, small-and-prayerful. To think at a bigger scale, think 'we,' not 'me'. The Church – not you, alone – is the interface between Christ and the enormous realities of the world that dwarf you. Build true community first, then collaborate to distribute God's resources together. Don't wait for perfection. Try, then learn from failure.

If we cannot take in information from our failures, we cannot 'iterate upward' – grow up spirally, or fail forward. Failure to build community is one 'failure of form' that impedes communication of Christ. Communication that is all 'top down,' or one-way, with no listening is a fail. Communication with empty signs, or through symbols that have lost meaning over time is a fail. (Don't throw out the signs – refill them!) Communication in technological forms that fight against the humanity of the audience, or contradict the message is a fail. Communication that is true, but unloving fails. Communication that ignores the forms of courtesy (please, please RSVP!), the dignity of persons,

---

[211] *Thinking in Systems*, Donella H. Meadows, Chelsea Green Publishing, 2008, pg. 165

or the lack of capacity in the recipient fails. Messaging systems that leave messages unanswered, or leave some parishioners off the newsletter list, or allow you to pretend to communicate without concern for actual results are failures. All this failure can tempt you toward condemnation – of yourself, or the flawed communicators around you, but "there is no condemnation in Christ Jesus"[212]

**Communication is Realizing Content and Context**

Communication is the dynamic process by which Word is realized in persons and persons are realized in words (acts, gestures, forms). The process involves you in Christ's work of restoring hope and humanity to man. Communicating Christ is a 'middlework' – recovery of the full dimensionality of persons, of the Church, and of culture by re-placement of Christ at the center of each. Christ's coming restores the metaphoric dimension of persons, the conversational and collaborative dimension of community, and the civic sphere of culture. Christ communicates not only Himself to you, but also you to yourself – inviting you, and the communities you inhabit, to become contexts wherein He may richly dwell, grow, and resound.

As you, as we, are becoming Christ-context, the Church grows organically into a structure that is vital to the economy of God's grace. Just as the body's blood is distributed by means of vascular structure, or the funds of a non-profit are distributed by means of its organizational structure, God offers us to the world as means for the distribution of His gifts. The Church is not 'external' to the

---

[212] Romans 8:1

hurting world, but 'deeply interior' to it by means of your presence. You are in the world, but not 'of' the structures and resources of the world.[213] Your freedom provides a fully open channel for the movement of God's loving, true, and beautiful response to whatever you encounter. Christ, Church, Person – each *is* and each *generates* the context necessary for personhood – for integral human development.

The Church as content – Bread for the world – is dying unless it is realized in new lives. The Church as context is emptying unless community life – *communio* – bubbles up within it. As a Christian – a form placed into the world – I am dead unless the Word sounds from within me. As a vessel – a form within-which – I am empty unless I am full of capacity-to-receive Christ, and those He loves.

If we place our hope of communicating Christ solely in the Truth, Goodness, and Beauty of that message, we will be disappointed to the extent hearers have no capacity to receive. If we, instead, create a pleasant atmosphere of warm feelings and ethical behavior, our communication will fail to generate the structural strength and transformation in those who enter the Church as context for immersive experience. Our audience needs *both* the with-strength of Sabbath practice, restored humanity, Mary's mothering, liturgy, and admission to loving community *and* the against-strength of doctrine, verbal skill and discipline, saintly role models, obligations and prohibitions, and demanding formalities.

The Church awaits the flourishing of your faith into a new way of living – the integration of desire and intellect into

---

[213] John 15:19

a capacity for good judgment that enables your freedom of action. Fr. Julian Carron calls us to "find a way of living the faith, within this social reality and pluralistic culture, such that others can perceive our presence not as something to defend themselves from, but as a contribution to the common good and their own personal good. We need a way of being present without a will to dominate or oppress, and at the same time *with* a commitment to living the faith in reality, in order to show the human benefit of belonging to Christ."[214] The world awaits the growing up of a community of adults who will condescend in love, collaborate with grace, and give freely in mercy to teach the perishing the way of personhood – the way of Christ.

**A Catholic Approach to Problems**

The call to 'do everything,' or even to 'dare to do something' suggests a Catholic approach to the enormity of the realities we currently face in the culture of death, disintegration and unbelief. A Catholic communication model offers a human-scale approach to the enormous realities: communicate Christ's response. When we communicate Christ, we voice His response to the realities we face together.

The first step in a Catholic approach to problems should be rejection of the problem-solution framework. Replace it with reality-response thinking and you'll begin to cultivate *actors in* instead of *managers of* the world. In *The Mind of the Maker*, Dorothy Sayers observed, "...the careless

---

[214] *Disarming Beauty*, Julián Carrón, University of Notre Dame Press, 2017, pg. 55

use of the words "problem" and "solution" can betray us into habits of thought that are not merely inadequate but false....They falsify our apprehension of life as disastrously as they falsify our apprehension of art."

"Problem solving" indicates a modern, mathematical approach. Math is great for finding 'answers' and 'solutions,' so it's understandable we would hope to deal with life's problematic realities in similar fashion. But math is an abstraction from concrete reality – great specifically because we can manipulate many real factors using its compact symbol system in a way that maps perfectly back onto that reality.

The simple flat tire, or broken lawnmower manage to resolve pretty quickly by that approach, but more complex realities seem to resist 'answers'. Just as a line drawing is a sufficient map for a simple route, 'problem' is an effective approach for simple realities. The problem with problems occurs as the level of complexity rises. The more factors of reality are involved in a 'situation,' 'crisis,' or 'issue,' the more a whole-human approach is needed to generate effective response. The more complex a set of factors, the less easily we can map them onto a simple graph, flow chart, or other model of reality. A model collapses '3D' wholeness into a '2D' space and attempts to find (or perhaps demands) a Solution, or Answer in that space. This approach may generate despair if the 'model world' is inadequate in its correspondence to the real world's complexity.

Consider, instead, what it would mean to respond to the realities you encounter. A response may or may not change the factors of reality, but brings the '2D' problem back into the '3D' perspective of a human free agent. Because you become an actor – a factor of reality yourself – you introduce the possibility of human creativity and of heavenly assistance. Your relationship to reality shifts, so the whole context shifts toward hope. There are realities so huge and complex that only the smallest possible response can help. 'Big' answers and solutions involve too much of the disordered reality and tend to make things worse. 'Hugeness' causes despair because 'huge' is not the scale of man, and man is the hope.

For any tension to be resolved, a creative resolution is needed that involves a 'point not on the plane,' 'help from above,' or a 'creative mind' that rises above to see and respond to the reality. Man's capacity to grasp wholes and generate wholes is enormous. No computer can quite compete, though more and more complex algorithms approach. Granted the computer can manipulate quantities with power, speed and accuracy that far outstrips its human operators. But man is needed to assimilate and interpret – to draw meaning from – the huge buckets of data computers can generate.

As a problem, reality looms disastrously large and impenetrable. Its name is Legion. It is faceless and it can't be beat. In actuality, we encounter those manifold factors of reality in person-sized doses to which we can actually respond constructively, lovingly, freely. Stepping down from the abstraction to the stage of action, we notice that, though all those factors are still present, our own tiny interior light now shows the many fibers of a dense and penetrable reality. We have but to take a tiny step, and the path begins to open.

Our approach should involve us as the Church, through membership in and collaboration with the Body of Christ, in designing responses to realities we face together. When I act, I should be conscious of being, as St. Pope John Paul called me, the 'way of the Church' – the means by which the Church acts in the world. This should mean that I respond, even if as an individual, in accord with the mind of the Church as expressed in her doctrines and teachings. To be able to respond, I must study and align with them. I must do the work of actually knitting the members of the Body together.

If we act or design initiatives together, we must first be a coherent, if imperfect, community. The world is to know us by our love for one another. Our unity with Christ is to be made visible as we serve others together. If we will not spend time weaving our real lives together into, as St. John Paul prayed during the Jubilee year, "communities of love, growing in Christ likeness," the frayed fabric of 'church' will not support the weight of the world's needs.

A human-scale means personal, person-centered. At the very least this means that we must keep (and help others to keep) the actual needs of real human persons at the center of all our initiatives in order to judge their effectiveness. This involves us in the turbulence and tension of competing goods instead of leaving us smugly invested in the subset of goods we find it easiest to give. We should be challenged to find the bent-ness, brokenness, need, pain, deformity, and worldliness of the world within the microcosm of self, family, and Catholic community. Only then will we beg God to send the comfort the world needs first *to*, then *through* us. God's strength is made perfect in our weakness (1 Cor. 12:9). We are not problems to be solved, but realities. God's response moves into the world through the subjective, intensely personal reality of one person, to another.

A Catholic approach will be educative. We must recognize the reality of the 'student's' limited capacity to receive, and condescend in love to communicate at his level – without violating the truth. This education must operate in two directions at once. We must 'teach' the Church about the realities we face – the cries for God's response that resonate through our own wounds. We must humbly learn what secular influencers are teaching, sift and honor all the truth we find there, and apply the constant, gentle pressure of interested Catholic critique. We can write bridges to the work of popular authors, interested and appreciative letters to the authors themselves, or study guides to popular works with Catholic commentary.

Our response should be slow, but not stuck: slow enough to begin and end in words fitly spoken, to wait while we wait upon the Lord, to waste time building relationship (among 'us' and with 'them'), to be formed into small (even symbolic) generative seeds of action that are filled with freedom and draped in love. Our response should involve our imaginations, because "God will do more than all we ask or imagine"[215] If Elon Musk can get rockets into orbit using 10x thinking, the Church might find its 100-fold thinkers and get them busy cultivating the infinite desire that corresponds to God's resources instead of to our own.

These are a few characteristics of a Catholic response to the realities we find ourselves facing together as the Body of Christ. They are meant to help the Church to cultivate and then mobilize free agents who understand themselves

---

[215] Ephesians 3:20

as vital channels of communication – of grace, of goods, of information, and of Christ. We actors distributed all over the world like nerve endings – keep the Church informed and responsive. Where we are, *real*-ly, light dawns and the Kingdom comes.

The work of the middle is to honor those before and above you, to collaborate with your fellow strugglers, and to turn in the condescension of love to teach and lift up others. Middlework – communication – is to bring down, digest, wrestle with, appropriate, enact, represent, and give what is good, true, and beautiful. It requires you be present before reality and persons, to develop your capacity for tension and resolution of tension, to practice and fail and learn from failure, and to relinquish your self-defenses and demands. Asked what would motivate you to engage in this work, Fr. Giussani replied, "…the *love of ourselves as destiny*, the affection for our own *destiny*…."

Attraction toward the possibility of richly inhabiting your own soul, of being known and loved to the uttermost degree, of living in eternal communion with God and His people draws you into the work of encounter with reality here and now. In the center of this work is a true fountain of life: Christ in the human person continually made new by movement toward full realization, bringing forth new forms from within Christ and His Church. You, free to receive and transmit the gifts of God by the power of the ever-moving Spirit to whom you are vessel and channel and beloved creation, are a life-giving, hope-inspiring, good-news-voicing, friend-following, form-building, love-mediating, reality-affirming, Christ-communicating work of art, co-operating in your own becoming! The people around you are waiting to discover these possibilities of personhood through you.

Made in the USA
Monee, IL
08 July 2023